HOW THE EBOOKS WORK

The eBooks are provided in EPUB file format. Please note that you will need an eBook reader installed on your device to open the file. Many devices come with this as standard, but you may still need to install one manually from Google Play.

The eBook content is identical to the content in the printed guide.

HOW TO DOWNLOAD THE WALKING EYE APP

1. Download the Walking Eye App from the App Store or Google Play.
2. Open the app and select the scanning function from the main menu.
3. Scan the QR code on this page – you will then be asked a security question to verify ownership of the book.
4. Once this has been verified, you will see your eBook in the purchased ebook section, where you will be able to download it.

Other destination apps and eBooks are available for purchase separately or are free with the purchase of the Insight Guide book.

TOP 10 ATTRACTIONS

CHIANTI
Vineyards cloak the fertile hills between Florence and Siena. See page 47.

DUOMO, FLORENCE
The cathedral is one of the best-known symbols of the city. See page 26.

LEANING TOWER OF PISA
The famous monument is the centrepiece of one of the most breathtaking piazzas in Italy. See page 55.

PIAZZA DEL CAMPO, SIENA
Its Torre di Mangia offers incredible views of the city. See page 61.

THE MAREMMA

Tuscany's southern coastline has many pretty beaches and resorts. See page 59.

UFFIZI GALLERY, FLORENCE

An almost dizzying collection of the Italian Renaissance's most revered paintings. See page 33.

SAN GIMIGNANO

A collection of beautifully preserved medieval towers gives this hill town a stunning skyline. See page 66.

THE GARFAGNANA

This mountainous area in the north is popular with hikers, climbers and canoeists. See page 53.

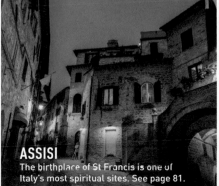

ASSISI

The birthplace of St Francis is one of Italy's most spiritual sites. See page 81.

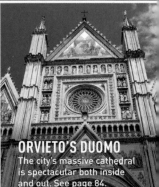

ORVIETO'S DUOMO

The city's massive cathedral is spectacular both inside and out. See page 84.

A PERFECT TOUR OF

Day 1

Historic towns
Drive west to Lucca on the A11, stopping at Pistoia for a stroll around its medieval alleyways and coffee in the central piazza. Continue on to Montecatini Terme and indulge in a spa treatment before lunch. Arrive in Lucca in time to seek out a traditional restaurant for some fine Tuscan cooking.

Day 2

Lucca
Hire a bicycle and ride along the top of the Renaissance walls then explore inside the walls starting from Piazza Napoleone – all the main sights are only a few minutes from here. Join the shoppers on Via Fillungo for some top-end retail therapy.

Day 3

Pisa
Continue along the A11 to the A12 for Pisa. Your first stop has to be Campo dei Meracoli, the green space graced by the Leaning Tower and the Duomo. From the Campo walk south passing through the most evocative part of the old city towards the river. Ideally book a hotel with a roof terrace overlooking the River Arno, and take an early evening riverside stroll before dinner.

Day 4–5

Viareggio
Enjoy breakfast on the roof terrace before travelling north on the SS1 to the seaside resort of Viareggio. The town's streets that run from the elegant beachside boulevard have plenty of hotels, pizzerias and shops. Take the chance to rejuvenate on the beach for a while.

NORTHERN TUSCANY

Day 7

Siena – Il Campo
Leave San Gimignano heading for Poggibonsi. Get on the Superstrada Firenze-Siena towards Italy's most perfect medieval city, Siena. In Siena first go to Il Campo and find a café where you can admire the buildings before visiting them. Next explore the sprawl of narrow streets near Il Campo, and find a bar for pre-dinner drinks.

Day 8

Siena – Duomo
Set aside the morning to visit Siena's magnificent cathedral. Don't overlook the cathedral's museum and climbing the steep stairway to a lookout with splendid views. After lunch take in Siena's many other sights, do a spot of shopping, and call in for ice cream at one of the city's best *gelateria*, La Vecchia Latteria (San Pietro 10).

Day 9

Chianti Country
The last day slowly meanders through Chianti Country. Leave Siena on the Chiantigiana road, calling in at Badia a Coltibuono, Radda, Greve and various wine estates dotted along the way (easy on the wine tasting if driving). Arrive in Florence in time for an evening meal.

Day 6

San Gimignano
Continue south on the SS1 skirting round. Take the SR68 west to Volterra, host to some splendid medieval buildings. From Volterra head to San Gimignano, perched on the hill in the distance. Park outside the walls and wonder the unspoiled streets seeking out the Collegiate and Palazzo Comunale. Stop over to appreciate this lovely town when the day-trippers have departed.

CONTENTS

INTRODUCTION

Visitors to Tuscany and Umbria will soon notice that the locals believe they live in the most ideal place on earth. The Florentines think of themselves as residents of one of the most prosperous cities in Italy, as caretakers of the greatest repository of art treasures in the Western world, and as speakers of the purest form of Italian. Elsewhere in Tuscany, you will meet people convinced they live in some of Europe's loveliest towns and villages, in Italy's most beautiful and bountiful region, produce some of the world's finest wines, and enjoy one of the most equable climates.

Then there are the Umbrians. They will have you convinced in no time that their landscapes of rolling hills and gentle valleys are imbued with a special spiritual quality. After all, St Francis, who may well be the world's most popular saint and who is in fact the patron saint of Italy, wandered this terrain and lived and died in the lovely, hill-clinging town of Assisi.

It would be difficult to argue with any of these claims. Florentines have indeed prospered since their merchants and trade guilds came of age in the Middle Ages. They do indeed have in their midst the greatest works of Michelangelo, Brunelleschi, Donatello and other masters of the Renaissance (which, of course, took root here). They can rightfully claim that their dialect evolved into modern-day Italian, under the influence of Dante and other Florentine writers. And the rest of Tuscany is truly beautiful, its wines are sublime, its climate is agreeable and its medieval towns fulfil just about any traveller's notions of what a European village should look like.

As for Umbria – well, take yourself to Assisi, wander its medieval streets, admire the Giotto frescoes in the St Francis basilica, and look out for the panorama of golden hills. You will then appreciate why people say the region is blessed with a spiritual aura.

TREASURES OF TUSCANY AND UMBRIA

What first strikes any traveller about Tuscany and Umbria is how attractive the landscapes are. The cypresses, olive trees and vineyards, the hilltops crowned with tile-roofed houses and proud towers, the tilled soil that glows amber in the slanting sun: these are the backdrops of the Renaissance paintings you have seen in galleries around the world, and you

Abbazia di Sant'Antimo, near Montalcino, Tuscany

will see the same scenes unfolding before your eyes as you travel the roads of these regions. The landscapes inspired the paintings, and the paintings in turn prepare you for what you will encounter.

Given the regions' representation in countless works of art, a traveller's perceptions of Tuscany and Umbria are usually of countryside punctuated now and then by medieval towns and of cities rising from fields and vineyards. In most cases the reality is not a disappointment. Some of the most memorable views in the world must include the towers of San Gimignano rising out of the golden fields as you approach the town from Volterra, the ochre-tiled roofs of Siena floating above the lush vineyards of Chianti, Orvieto cascading across a mountaintop above the undulating Umbrian countryside below, and, of course, Brunelleschi's magnificent dome signalling your approach to Florence before the rest of the city comes into view.

Sunflowers in the Siena countryside

Going beyond the lay of the land, these two regions are also home to some of Italy's most important works of art, highly appraised cuisines and lively cultures that continue centuries-old traditions. It seems that everywhere you turn there is another artistic work by a Renaissance master, or a medieval church. The Tuscans and Umbrians, who have grown up among such beauty, hold festivals that honour their great past, whether parades in historical costume or glorifying quotidian or specific events of the 14th and 15th centuries.

INTO MODERNITY

Modern-day progress has left its mark here as well. While these regions remain primarily rural, as they have been since Etruscan times, fewer people work the land now than even 50 years ago. The *contadini*, farmers who for centuries tilled the soil, are now either landowners themselves or have given up farming altogether. Many now commute from their land to jobs in the city, others have converted their farmhouses into holiday homes. Industry has encroached on the countryside (especially in the valleys around Florence), and many towns and cities have outgrown their original walls and are now surrounded by modern suburbs.

Tuscans and Umbrians, however, are never too far removed from their rural roots. A walk in the country is still the favoured pastime of many city dwellers, and a patch of tomatoes or a chicken coop occupies the corner of many apartment terraces and suburban plots. In many places, careful zoning keeps sprawl to well-defined sectors – even in ever-expanding cities like Florence and Perugia you can still look from a belvedere over scenery that is primarily rural. Part of the pleasure of travelling here is seeing how well the rural and the urban, the old and the new, coexist.

In the post-World War II years, Tuscans and Umbrians have learned how to interact with another modern phenomenon – tourism. Not that travellers hadn't long ago discovered the pleasures of Florence and the other art-rich Tuscan and Umbrian cities. Read E.M. Forster's *A Room with a View* to see the profound effect Florence had on Edwardians and other travellers before them. Mass tourism is a different matter, however, and Florence in particular needs to manage it with care, so that its character is not spoiled.

Visit Florence and other popular towns such as San Gimignano outside their busiest summer months, and you will have a far more relaxing experience. If you do visit during high season, simply head for the quieter places. One of the best antidotes to summertime Florence is a retreat to hilltop Fiesole, where you will be rewarded with a stunning view, a glimpse of Roman ruins and a cooling breeze.

Everyone seems to find somewhere in Tuscany and Umbria that they fall in love with, and often it is not a famous sight, but a little-known out-of-the-way spot. You too may find a place that stays with you for ever, and to which you will want to return again and again.

Free culture

Thanks to a government initiative called *Domenica al museo*, most state-run museums (and archaeological areas) are free the first Sunday of each month across Italy.

A BRIEF HISTORY

The first chapter of Tuscan history belongs to Etruscan tribes known as the Tusci, from whom the region took its name. The origins of the Etruscans are shrouded in mystery, but most modern scholars believe they migrated from Eastern Europe over the Alps, and represented the flowering of the early Italic tribes. These tribes moved into Umbria, pushing out their chief enemy, the Umbri, the agricultural tribe who in turn gave their name to that region. Around 3,000 years ago an advanced Etruscan culture was thriving in the hilly terrain that surrounds present-day Volterra in western Tuscany. Much of what they left behind is now on display in Volterra's Museo Etrusco

Roman theatre, Volterra

Guarnacci (see page 68). These early tribes left their mark in other ways too. It was the Etruscans who introduced the system of artificial irrigation and the Umbrians who reared the white cattle for which the region is still renowned.

Guarnacci (see page 68).

Pieces of history

Archaeologists have pieced together what they know of the Etruscan civilisation by analysing their ruins and artefacts. Some key Tuscan sites with evidence of the Etruscans include Fiesole, the Maremma, Volterra and Cortona.

THE ROMAN PERIOD

Rome annexed Etruria in 351BC, and, over the next two centuries, built four great Roman roads across the territory, part of the massive road-building programme that was to transform Italy. The new roads avoided the great Etruscan cities, which slowly fell into decline, allowing the new Roman cities such as Pistoriae (Pistoia) to grow in importance. New colonies were founded at Ansedonia, Fiesole, Roselle, Populonia, Volterra, Luni and Lucca. The cultural identity of the Etruscans was gradually absorbed into that of the Romans, a process that accelerated in 91BC when Roman citizenship was extended to the Etruscans.

By 59BC, when Julius Caesar established the colony of Florentia as a kind of retirement community for veterans (a clever way to maintain order in outlying provinces), the Etruscans were long gone from both Tuscany and Umbria, overrun by the joint menace of the Romans from the south and the Gauls from the north. But the Romans learned many things from the Etruscans – principally the Tuscan arch, which they developed as a key element in their extraordinary aqueducts, bridges and buildings.

By creating the roads and major cities of Tuscany, the Romans left a permanent imprint on the landscape. A

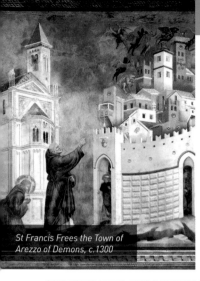

St Francis Frees the Town of Arezzo of Demons, c.1300

millennium later, the ruins of their great bridges, amphitheatres and city walls would be the inspiration for the next great blossoming of Italian culture: Tuscany's coming of age, the Renaissance.

After invasions by Goths and, later, Byzantine armies put an end to control from Rome, much of Tuscany re-emerged under the stable influence of the Lombards.

CHRISTIANITY AND MEDIEVAL CLASHES

Long before the Roman Empire went into decline in the late 5th century AD, Christianity had gained a foothold in the region. The first monastery was established near Spoleto in the 1st century AD; around AD250 St Minias became the first Christian martyr in Florence, and the city, which became capital of the province of Tuscia in the 3rd century, was the seat of a bishopric early in the following century. St Benedict, born in Umbria in 480, founded one of the first religious orders, and another son of Umbria, Francis of Assisi, born in 1182, would become one of Italy's most beloved saints. During the medieval period the pilgrims travelling along the Via Francigena between Rome and France meant that Christianity brought wealth and development to the whole area.

Though prosperous, the region was far from peaceful. Unrest rippled across the land with the Guelf–Ghibelline struggles, in essence a scramble for power between the temporal leaders of the Holy Roman Empire (the Ghibellines) and the Pope and his supporters (the Guelfs). Florence's sympathies were with the Guelfs; most of the city's rivals, including Pisa and Siena, were Ghibelline. Florence attained the ascendancy as the fortunes of Pisa, once a great maritime power, waned when Genoa triumphed at sea, and as Cosimo de' Medici, scion of Europe's greatest banking family, led Florence to final victory over its one remaining rival, Siena, in 1557.

In the Papal States' quest for power, popes sent armies to Umbria to conquer its proud hill towns. Perugia, the wealthiest, most powerful and most independent of them all, mounted the greatest resistance. In the 16th century, the Baglioni clan, the city's ruling family, went so far as to try to assassinate a papal legate. The papacy retaliated, first by increasing the salt tax (avoidance of this usurious yet frequently used form of

⊘ ST FRANCIS OF ASSISI

Nobody embodies Christian teaching quite so appealingly as St Francis, Umbria's most famous son, born in Assisi in 1182. When he was 27, Francis received a call to give his life to God; he renounced his sizeable inheritance, dressed himself in sackcloth and began to preach. He urged his growing body of followers to renounce material possessions and pledge obedience to God and, in a refreshing departure from the fire and brimstone that had characterised much Church teaching until then, to appreciate the beauty of the natural world, which was God's creation. Francis founded an order and took his message across Europe and to the Holy Land with the Crusaders. He died on the floor of his hut in Assisi in 1226 and was canonised two years later. Assisi has been an important point of pilgrimage ever since.

taxation is the reason Umbrian bread is still made without salt) and eventually by taking over the city and, for good measure, levelling the Baglioni palaces and the surrounding neighbourhood. (As you ascend from the city's underground parking lots, a series of passageways takes you past these evocative ruins.)

THE RENAISSANCE

Amid all this strife, Florentines were engaging in a frenzy of activity that would pull Western civilisation out of the Dark Ages. The Renaissance took root in Florence in the early 15th century, under the patronage of the powerful Medici clan, who, with some bloody interruptions, would continue to rule Florence, and most of Tuscany, until the middle of the 18th century.

In March 1436, Florence celebrated the completion of the dome that crowns its cathedral. The construction of this massive

⊘ THE MEDICI

Decidedly *the* most important family of the Renaissance, the Medici made their fortune as bankers and craftily positioned themselves among the city's decision-makers, often without even holding an official government office. Cosimo, *Il Vecchio* ('the Elder') earned himself the title *pater patriae* ('father of his country') and hereby started the family's dynasty. Perhaps the most famous Medici was Lorenzo, *Il Magnifico* ('the Magnificent'), who was a huge patron of Renaissance artists and a master of diplomacy. In the years following his death, however, the Medici's fate took an unfortunate turn, as the family was eventually run out of town for a questionable political manoeuvre in a war with France. In 1512 the Medici regained control of the city and ruled Florence as the grand dukes of Tuscany until 1743.

drum was one of the great architectural achievements of the Renaissance. The dome still rises high above Florence as if to announce that, yes, this is where the Renaissance first blossomed.

At every turn in the city you can trace the development of this movement that enabled people to look at the world in an enlightened way. In the Uffizi, the art gallery Florence founded in the 16th century, you will see how Uccello became one of the first painters to master that great Renaissance contribution, perspective; and in the church of San Lorenzo you may notice how the architect Brunelleschi introduced a new order to spatial relationships.

Lorenzo de' Medici, in Gozzoli's *The Journey of the Magi*

In the Accademia, you need only look at that most famous of all Renaissance sculptures, Michelangelo's *David*, to see how the Renaissance revolutionised the way sculptors looked at the human form. And in the Bargello you can appreciate how Donatello's wonderful marble *St George* introduced a new realism, depicting the saint as a human being, alive and ready for action.

Umbria did not embrace the Renaissance with the same fervour as its neighbour, Tuscany, but there was an artistic flowering here as well, as a glimpse of Giotto's frescoes depicting the life of St Francis (28 panels in the church dedicated to the saint in Assisi) will testify.

FROM UNIFICATION TO WORLD WAR II

Despite these amazing accomplishments, the citizens of Florence and the rest of Tuscany slumbered through the post-Renaissance years as a backwater, a pawn to greater European powers. In 1860, after more than a century of capable rule by the House of Lorraine, Tuscany joined forces with Piedmont as part of a united Italy. Florence, in fact, served briefly as the Italian capital from 1865 to 1871.

In Umbria, papal control continued almost uninterrupted until the unification of Italy in 1860, and the benign neglect with which the region was administered may well explain the unchanged state of Umbrian hill towns well into the 19th century. When the new Italian state took control, towns like Perugia welcomed their freedom from papal oppression.

Both regions have seen great sorrow in their more recent history. The absence of old bridges across the Arno attests to the role Tuscany played in World War II. Some of the major battles in the European theatre took place in and around Florence in the summer of 1944, when the Germans entrenched themselves along the Arno and in the surrounding mountains as the Allies advanced. The Germans retreated in August, but not before blowing up the city's beloved bridges, leaving only the Ponte Vecchio intact.

RECENT DEVELOPMENTS

The world's attention turned to the Arno again in November 1966, when the river burst its banks and floodwaters ravaged many of the city's art treasures. Restoration efforts continued for decades, fuelled by the Florentines' belief that they are protectors of the Renaissance heritage. These same custodial efforts came into play again in May 1993, when a car bomb ripped through parts of the Uffizi galleries; within

Florence's Ponte alle Grazie was rebuilt in 1953 after being destroyed by the Germans

months, the damage had been repaired and the museum had reopened.

Umbria, after finally reaching an unprecedented level of prosperity in the last few decades of the 20th century, was struck by disaster in 1997, when earthquakes shook the peaceful region, killing four and causing extensive damage. Nevertheless, restoration was remarkably rapid, with many churches and buildings reopening just five years later. Northwest Tuscany also suffered disaster in October 2011, when severe flash-floods tragically caused people to lose their lives and their homes.

The two regions continue to rely on two main sources of income and livelihood: tourism and agriculture. Tuscany's wines and olive oil are famous the world over, and Umbria, though often overshadowed by its neighbour, produces wheat and tobacco, as well as olives and grapes.

Keeping in touch with the past

Despite the many advantages it brings to both regions, tourism has brought problems as well. By creating large parking lots underground and in the valleys below hilltop cities, Umbria has been especially successful at making its cities traffic-free without causing too much discomfort to local motorists. And in an effort to cut congestion and pollution, the first of three tram lines was opened in Florence in February 2010.

For a long time Florence had run the risk of becoming a sealed monument but following the election of charismatic mayor Matteo Renzi, the city showed signs of moving forward. The expansion of the Uffizi, with new rooms opened at the end of 2011, is testament to the progress made. The current mayor, Dario Nardella, has vowed to be just as progressive but without harming the identity of the city. No doubt in the years to come both Tuscany and Umbria will continue to strive to find the best ways to face modern challenges whilst preserving the vast treasures of their past.

HISTORICAL LANDMARKS

800–500BC Etruscan civilisation thrives in the region.

59BC Rome sets up an outpost called Florentia.

Mid-6th–9th century Lombards and Franks control much of what is now Tuscany and Umbria.

1226 St Francis of Assisi, patron saint of Italy, dies.

13th–14th century Conflicts between Guelfs and Ghibellines divide loyalties; most towns are independent, free communities.

1250–1600 The flowering of the Renaissance.

14th century Florence, growing more powerful, conquers Arezzo, Volterra and other cities and towns.

14–17th century Umbrian cities come under the power of the papacy.

1348 The plague severely depletes the populations of both Florence and Siena.

1436 The dome of Florence's cathedral is completed.

1495 Inspired by ascetic monk Savonarola, Florentines burn material possessions on 'Bonfires of the Vanities' in Piazza della Signoria.

1498 Savonarola is burned at the stake.

1504 Michelangelo completes *David*.

1581 The Uffizi Gallery opens.

1860s Tuscany and Umbria become part of unified Italy. Florence serves as capital from 1865 to 1871.

1944 Germans destroy all the bridges in Florence, except the Ponte Vecchio.

1966 Floodwaters ravage Florentine art treasures.

1993 A bomb rips through the Uffizi.

1997 Earthquakes shake Umbria, destroying frescoes in Assisi's basilica.

2001 The Tower of Pisa reopens to the public.

2002 The euro replaces the lira.

2007 Work begins in January on the expansion of the Uffizi.

2011 Devastating floods in northeast Tuscany.

2014 Mayor of Florence Matteo Renzi is elected Prime Minister of Italy, holding office until 2016.

2018 The first stage of the restoration of Michelangelo's tomb in Florence is completed.

Statue of Dante Alighieri outside Santa Croce, Florence

WHERE TO GO

When it comes to determining how to plan the logistics of your travels in Tuscany and Umbria, you are both blessed and cursed. For better or worse, and to understate the case, there is just so much to see. Fortunately, the regions are compact enough that you can travel through them with ease, and the road and train networks are excellent.

One approach is to divide the regions into sections to be explored in forays from various principal bases. From Florence you can explore Fiesole, Pistoia, Lucca, Pisa and the Chianti countryside to the south, as well as the lesser-known Mugello to the north. From Siena you can follow a spur of the Apennines that separates the central valleys of Italy from the Mediterranean coast, and explore a string of hill towns that include San Gimignano, Volterra and Montepulciano. The centuries-old university town of Perugia is a perfect base from which to set out for Gubbio, Assisi, Spoleto, Orvieto... and the list could go on.

FLORENCE

Florence ❶ has been variously described as the most beautiful city in Italy; a 'city of stone', imposing and difficult to penetrate; the artistic and humanistic seat of the Renaissance; and one of the most popular tourist destinations in the world. It should come as no surprise, then, that its history is as varied as its current incarnations.

Florence was founded by Julius Caesar as a colony for old soldiers in 59BC, and traces of this orderly era remain in the neat layout of blocks between the Duomo and the Piazza della Signoria. The city muddled through the Roman era as a pleasant backwater, survived the Dark Ages intact, and then, through the wars, revolutions and religious turmoil of the next centuries, began to prosper. Under the generous patronage of the ruling Medici family, sculptors, painters, poets and architects thrived. A surprising number of their works have remained in Florence, kept there by a clause in the will of Anna Maria Ludovica, the last Medici, who in 1743 stipulated that none of the family's vast holdings was ever to leave Florence. Her wishes have largely been respected, and Florence today provides the visitor with an amazing concentration of the legacy of the remarkable minds of the Renaissance.

All this cultural heritage may sound a bit daunting, but take heart. Sights are close to each other, and all are just a few minutes' walk from the Piazza del Duomo and its cathedral, the visual and geographic centre of the city.

Subtle changes are taking place in Florence – more pedestrianised zones, the rejuvenation of the Arno riverbanks – but the city remains the Florence we all know and love.

PIAZZA DEL DUOMO

The **Duomo** Ⓐ (more properly, Santa Maria del Fiore; Mon–Wed, Fri 10am–5pm, Thu 10am–4.30pm, Sat 10am–4.45pm, Sun 1.30–4.45pm, times subject to change due to events; www.operaduomo.firenze.it) was more than a century in the making. Begun at the end of the 13th century, it was not completed until the late 1460s. The original plans were drawn up by Arnolfo di Cambio, who envisioned the largest cathedral in the world, with an octagonal

View from the top

Queues form at a doorway on the north side of the Duomo's exterior to climb the stairs leading to the top of the dome. The summit provides an extraordinary panorama of the city.

Marble collection – the Baptistery, Duomo and Campanile

crossing measuring nearly 46m (150ft) across, to be topped by an enormous dome. Just eight years after construction began, Arnolfo died. A series of architects continued his work, completing the body of the church and the drum for the dome by 1418.

The architects faced a considerable structural challenge – how to erect a 91m (300ft) high dome over the vast crossing. Into the bickering community of architects and masons stepped fledgling architect Filippo Brunelleschi, who said he could build it, and without using expensive scaffolding, but declined to say how. He was given the job, and confounded sceptics with the elegance of his solution. He designed the dome to be built in two shells of brick, arranged in cantilevered rings so that, as the structure rose, each layer of masonry would support the one above. The Duomo remains one of the masterpieces of the Renaissance, visible from every point in the city, and providing fine views from every angle.

The exterior of the Duomo is clad in patterned marble of three hues – green, white and red – but the overly elaborate facade is actually a 19th-century construct. On the north facade is Porta della Mandorla; its relief, *The Assumption of the Virgin*, was executed by Nanni di Banco in the 15th century.

The interior is vast, almost austere in its lineaments. The cathedral has accommodated 10,000 worshippers in its bare, grey-and-white interior. Busts of Brunelleschi and Giotto are placed near the entrance. On the wall of the left aisle is a frescoed memorial to Sir John Hawkwood, the English mercenary who was a battle-winning captain of the Florentine army from 1377 until his death; it was painted by Paolo Uccello in the 15th century. Near the end of the aisle is a 15th-century painting by Domenico di Michelino, *Dante Explaining the Divine Comedy*, in which the Duomo is placed in clear opposition to Hell and Purgatory – a juxtaposition whose meaning must have been clear to a contemporary Florentine. In the right aisle are steps leading down to the old Santa Reperata church, around which the Duomo was built. In 1972 excavators found a funerary slab inscribed with Brunelleschi's name; it can now be seen through a gate.

The largest work of art in the Duomo is a fresco on the underside of the dome depicting *The Last Judgement*; the work was designed by the Florentine architect Giorgio Vasari, executed by his student Frederico Zuccari in the late 16th century, and cleaned and restored in the late 20th. In his design, Brunelleschi added iron hooks to facilitate cleaning and even spaces where canteens were installed for the builders. The gallery provides an excellent vantage point to view seven circular stained-glass windows by Uccello, Castagno, Donatello and Ghiberti.

The Duomo tends to overshadow two other noteworthy buildings on the piazza – the Campanile and the Baptistery. The **Campanile** (daily 8.15am–7pm) is one of the loveliest belfries in Italy. Begun by Giotto in 1334 and finished after his death, it has been hard-hit by atmospheric pollution, and many of its sculptural reliefs are copies. The originals, including works by Donatello, are in the Museo dell'Opera del Duomo (see page 30). A terrace on top offers a view of the city.

The **Baptistery** (Mon–Fri 8.15–10.15am, 11.15am–7.30pm, Sat 8.15am–6.30pm, Sun 8.15am–1.30pm) dates from the 6th century, which makes it the oldest building in Florence. It may originally have been a temple to the Roman god of war, Mars; certainly, it was once the city's main church and the site of a kind of mass baptism every March for all Florentine children born during the preceding year. The building is most famous for its gilded bronze doors, the originals of which are on view in the Opera del Duomo museum.

The Baptistery's magnificent gilded bronze east doors, the so-called 'Gates of Paradise'

The doors on the south were cast in 1336 by Andrea Pisano, who succeeded Giotto in overseeing the Campanile; their 28 compartments depict the story of John the Baptist, patron saint of Florence (for the edification of his audience). Some 60 years later, the city organised a competition to choose a sculptor for the north door. The surfeit of talent it attracted included Brunelleschi, Donatello and a 22-year-old Tuscan artist called Lorenzo Ghiberti. Ghiberti and Brunelleschi were deemed equally worthy by the judges, and it was suggested that they work together. But Brunelleschi chose instead to study dome-making in Rome, and Ghiberti worked alone.

His achievement is considerable. The north doors show scenes from the lives of Christ, the Evangelists, and the Doctors of the Church; one can see the sculptor's skill grow with each subsequent panel. Pleased with his work, the city commissioned Ghiberti to cast doors for the east wall; he began work on those in 1425. There, in his masterpiece, he altered his earlier conception somewhat, forming 10 large panels to show scenes from the Old Testament. The art is vigorous and concise; the masterful low relief extends far into the background. Michelangelo, when he saw the work, called it the Gates of Paradise.

Inside, the Baptistery is stately, with its granite Roman columns and 13th-century mosaic ceiling and floors. The empty octagonal space in the centre was the site of the baptism of all of Florence's children.

Much of the art that once adorned the cathedral and the Baptistery is now housed in the **Museo dell'Opera del Duomo** (daily 9am–7pm, closed 1st Tue of each month) on the north-eastern side of the piazza. Set out in 25 rooms over 3 levels, the recently restructured museum offers a stunning light space to exhibit more than 750 works of art. The central courtyard of the museum displays Ghiberti's original Gates of Paradise. All

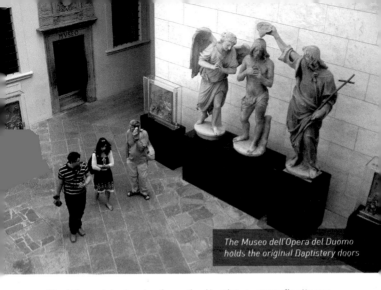

The Museo dell'Opera del Duomo holds the original Baptistery doors

10 of the original gates from the Baptistery were finally reunited in the museum in September 2012 after 27 years of restoration. In a room of quiet isolation is Michelangelo's second *Pietà*, partly finished by one of his students, and intended for the artist's own funerary monument. The first floor houses two *cantorie* (choir balconies) dating from the 15th century. One is by Donatello and the other by Luca della Robbia.

PIAZZA DELLA SIGNORIA

From the Duomo, Via dei Calzaiuoli leads south to the expansive **Piazza della Signoria**, the historical centre of Florence and once the political centre as well. Savonarola, the Dominican friar whose fiery, puritanical oratory against worldly excesses gripped Florence in the late 15th century, staged the Bonfire of the Vanities here, a huge conflagration of fine clothes, art and books. Savonarola was himself burned here, just a few years later.

Today the piazza is framed by beautiful statues, including a copy of Michelangelo's *David*. It also accommodates several cafés. At the south end is the **Loggia dei Lanzi**, a statue-filled portico built in the late 14th century. Pride of place is taken by two masterpieces of Renaissance sculpture: Giambologna's *Rape of the Sabine Women* and Donatello's *Judith and Holofernes*. Facing onto the piazza, Gucci sealed its 90th anniversary in 2011 with the unveiling of the **Gucci Museo**, a homage to this Florentine success story. The museum has now been transformed into the Gucci Garden, a space with galleries, a boutique, cinema and restaurant.

The **Palazzo Vecchio** Ⓑ (Fri–Wed 9am–7pm, Thu 9am–2pm, later at peak times; www.florence-museum.com) also fronts on the square. Originally designed by Arnolfo di Cambio, with additions made over the next few centuries, it serves as the seat of the municipal government. The building is inevitably described as 'fortress-like' but actually contains some odd and lovely rooms that are open to the public. The huge Salone dei Cinquecento is panelled with 16th-century frescoes by Giorgio Vasari celebrating Cosimo de' Medici's military triumphs; beyond the salon is a windowless chamber built for Cosimo's son, Francesco, and decorated to reflect his interest in alchemy.

Upstairs are several rooms of note – Eleanor of Toledo's chapel decorated by Bronzini in frescoes glazed with tempera, and the Sala dei Gigli, with a lovely 15th-century ceiling. The attached Cancelleria was

Avoid the queues

Queues for the Uffizi and Accademia can be extremely long, especially during spring and summer. To make a reservation for a timed entrance go online at www.b-ticket.com/b-ticket/uffizi. Please note a small charge will be added to the price of the ticket.

once Niccolò Machiavelli's office; the adjacent room is adorned with maps that show the known world *circa* 1563.

GALLERIA DEGLI UFFIZI

A few steps away is the **Galleria degli Uffizi**  (Tue–Sun 8.15am–6.50pm; www.uffizi.it), which contains an unrivalled collection of Renaissance art, with masterworks by Giotto, Uccello, Botticelli, da Vinci, Michelangelo, Raphael, Titian, Caravaggio and others. One could easily spend a week here. While that is probably not possible, certain treasures are not to be missed in even the shortest visit. A walk through the Uffizi gallery provides a fine overview of the flowering of European culture. Although some rooms may be closed and some paintings shifted, the following should give you the approximate locations of the major works.

On the second floor in Room 2 is the *Ognissanti Maestà*, the *Madonna Enthroned*, painted by Giotto in 1310, one of the first renderings of this subject to present it realistically. Room 3 contains the *Annunciation* by Simone Martini, with the Virgin regarding the angel from a field of gold. In the centre of Room 7 is a diptych by Piero della Francesca depicting Federico da Montefeltro, the Duke of Urbino, and his wife, painted in profile and gazing at each other still. Rooms 10 to 14, now one large hall, are devoted to Botticelli; note especially his *Birth of*

Crowds outside the Uffizi

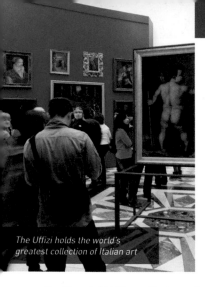
The Uffizi holds the world's greatest collection of Italian art

Venus, in which the newly born goddess floats to shore on a shell. Room 15 contains early works by Leonardo da Vinci, including an *Annunciation* painted in 1472.

Succeeding rooms offer works by Albrecht Dürer, among others. In Room 25, the centrepiece is Michelangelo's *Tondo Doni* (Holy Family) – his only finished easel painting. Room 28 is devoted to works by Titian, chief among them the *Venus of Urbino*, a fleshy and provocative nude. Rooms 31 to 34 display the works of artists from Italy's Veneto region, including Tintoretto's *Leda* and Paolo Veronese's *Annunciation*. Room 44 has several Rembrandt portraits, notably his haunting *Self-Portrait as an Old Man*. Windows provide views of the city, and the halls are lined with self-portraits by Raphael, Velásquez and Ingres, among others. On the first floor (which formerly held the archives) are the Caravaggio rooms dedicated to the master of *chiaroscuro* and other 'Caravaggesque' painters.

Still on the first floor, the nine Red Rooms are rich in masterpieces and artworks of important artists. These, together with the eight Blue Rooms dedicated to foreign painters of the 16th, 17th and 18th centuries, corroborates the progress made to expand the Uffizi in more recent years.

The pleasant roof-terrace bar is a good place to take a break and enjoy the view.

AROUND PIAZZA DELLA REPUBBLICA

The **Piazza della Repubblica**, entered on the western side through a grand triumphal arch, was built in the late 19th century on the site of the Roman forum, the first step in the planned redevelopment of the city. The 14th-century Mercato Vecchio and a jumble of medieval streets were cleared as part of a modernisation programme that, for whatever reason, was halted before the rest of the city could be changed. Today, lined with smart cafés that are packed at lunchtime with workers from the surrounding offices, it is the only modern intrusion in the heart of the city.

Southeast of the square you'll find **Orsanmichele ⑪** (daily 10am–4.30pm; free; www.bargellomusei.beniculturali.it), certainly one of the oddest churches extant. It was built to serve as a granary in 1337, then was turned into a chapel when an image of the Madonna inside became celebrated for performing miracles. The niches on the exterior are decorated with statues of saints by Verrocchio, Ghiberti and Donatello, commissioned by the city's merchant guilds (now replaced by casts). The original sculptures can be seen in the first-floor museum (Mon 10am–4.30pm, Sat 10am–12.30pm).

To the south is the **Mercato Nuovo** (New Market, also called the Straw Market), where stalls are piled high with leather articles, painted trays and other typically Florentine goods. More enticing than most of the merchandise is *Il Porcellino*, a bronze copy of a reclining boar (the original is in the Uffizi); even haughty Florentines pause to rub the beast's well-worn snout, an act that is said to ensure good luck.

From the Mercato Nuovo, follow Via Porta Rossa

Atmospheric amble

Between the Duomo and Piazza della Signoria, east of Orsanmichele, is an area of atmospheric medieval streets, well worth a wander.

west, and you'll find the **Palazzo Davanzati** (Mon–Fri 8.15am–1.50pm, Sat–Sun 1.15–6.50pm, closed 1st, 3rd and 5th Mon, 2nd and 4th Sun of the month; www.bargellomusei.beniculturali.it). This 14th-century structure, with a somewhat intimidating facade, was once a family's residence. The colourful interior has been restored to show how the palace would have looked. The fresco cycle in the bedroom and the vivid Sala dei Pappagalli are notable.

In the next piazza over is the **Palazzo Strozzi** (daily 10am–8pm, Thu until 11pm; charge; www.palazzostrozzi.org). Built in the late 15th to early 16th century for the Strozzi family, it now hosts important art exhibits and has a delightful courtyard. The Strozzina, a contemporary art space under the courtyard, has an expanding programme of a variety of international exhibitions.

THE BARGELLO AND SANTA CROCE

The east side of the historic centre starts at the **Bargello** **E** (Mon–Fri 8.15am–1.50pm, Sat–Sun until 4.50pm closed 2nd and 4th Sun, 1st, 3rd and 5th Mon of the month; www.bargellomusei.beniculturali.it). This imposing structure was built in the mid-13th century, and for many years was the seat of the magistrate of Florence, and the site of numerous trials, with public executions in the courtyard. Restored in the 19th century, this is now an elegant spot.

The great hall of the **Museo Nazionale del Bargello** contains works by Michelangelo and his school. He carved the classically inspired *Bacchus* when just 22 years old, and the bust of *Brutus* after the murder of the autocratic Duke Alessandro de' Medici in 1537, as a statement of his republican principles. A stairway leads from the courtyard to the loggia, home to a series of bronze birds cast by Giambologna for a Medici villa. A doorway to the right opens into a 14th-century salon

dominated by works by Donatello. Most notable are his bronze of *David*, and his figure of *Saint George*, carved in 1416.

In a rear corner are two bronze panels that Ghiberti and Brunelleschi entered in the competition to cast the doors of the Baptistery; the theme is the *Sacrifice of Isaac*. The remaining rooms on this floor contain a wide-ranging array of decorative art, including ivory carvings from Europe and the Middle East. On the second floor, the Sala dei Bronzetti holds a remarkable display of small Renaissance bronzes.

From the Bargello, go south into Piazza San Firenze, and turn left onto Borgo dei Greci, which will take you all the way to the church of **Santa Croce**  (Mon–Sat 9.30am–5.30pm, Sun 2–5.30pm; www.santacroceopera.it), the Franciscan outpost in the city, said to be founded by St Francis himself. It was begun at the end of the 13th century and consecrated in the mid-15th; the facade was not completed until 1857.

Today the huge interior serves as the final resting place for many prominent Florentines, including Michelangelo (first tomb on the right aisle, designed by Vasari), Dante Alighieri (monument only; his bones are in Ravenna) and Galileo (on the opposite side). The frescoes in the Cappella Peruzzi and the Cappella Bardi, on the right side of the church, are by Giotto. Their poor condition is partly because he painted onto dry plaster instead of wet, and partly because of vandalism – in the 18th century, they were whitewashed over, then retouched in the 19th. Nonetheless, Giotto's depictions of scenes from the lives of St John the Evangelist, St John the Baptist and St Francis are infused with

☉ FLORENCE MARKETS

Markets are a wonderful place to witness the daily activity of the townspeople. Florence is one of the best cities for markets selling fresh foods and local goods. While bargaining can sometimes be used when purchasing local goods such as scarves, jewellery, leather goods or other clothes, it is not recommended that you try it when buying from the food stands.

Mercato Centrale. Mon–Sat 7am–2pm, Sat also 4–7pm. Fresh fruit, vegetables, meat, fish and other local culinary specialities. Under cover in Via dell'Ariento.

Mercato del Porcellino. Mon–Sat 9am–6.30pm. Local goods at Piazza del Mercato Nuovo.

San Lorenzo street market. Tue–Sat approximately 8am–7/7.30pm. A huge area of stands selling local goods from near Piazza San Lorenzo to Via dell'Ariento.

Mercato di Sant'Ambrogio. Mon–Sat 7am–2pm. The second-largest fresh food market in the city, partially undercover, at Piazza Ghiberti near Chiesa Sant'Ambrogio.

his vigour and humanity; above the entrance to the Bardi Chapel is the powerful *Saint Francis Receiving the Stigmata*. Note also Donatello's wooden crucifix in the chapel at the end of the left transept, criticised by Brunelleschi for making Christ look like a mere peasant, but peculiarly resonant to modern eyes.

Autumnal local produce

SANTA MARIA NOVELLA TO THE ACCADEMIA

North of the centre, near the main station, is **Santa Maria Novella**  (Mon–Thu 9am–5.30pm, Fri 11am–5.30pm, Sat 9am–5pm, Sun 1–5pm), a 14th-century Dominican church with an oddly cheerful green, white and pink marble facade. The interior contains some lovely frescoed chapels, especially the sanctuary behind the main altar, created by Ghirlandaio and his assistants, including a young Michelangelo. The adjoining museum, in the cloisters, has frescoes by Paolo Uccello. His depiction of the biblical flood was damaged by the 1966 floods, but his mastery of perspective can still be appreciated.

A few blocks east is **San Lorenzo** (Mon–Sat 10am–5.30pm, Sun 1.30–5.30pm, closed Sun Nov–Mar; www.opera-medicealaurenziana.org), the Medici's local parish church and the oldest in Florence. Their patronage funded a rebuilding of the original 4th-century structure in the 15th century, designed by Brunelleschi. His skill is evident in the Old Sacristy, a

lovely bit of Renaissance architecture, decorated with ter-
racotta designed by Donatello. The **Medici Chapels**, entered
behind the church, contain a gloomy and ornate collection of
Medici tombs. The highlight is the New Sacristy, designed by
Michelangelo in 1520; note especially his carved tombs for
Lorenzo, Duke of Urbino, and Giuliano, Duke of Nemours.

In **San Lorenzo street market** just beyond the piazza, you
may, with a sharp eye and strength to fend off aggressive
sales pitches, be able to find some excellent leather goods
and clothing. North of the church is an interesting commercial
enterprise, the **Mercato Centrale**, the city's major food market.

Leaving the market, walk onto Via Cavour and take a left to
reach the **Palazzo Medici Riccardi** (Thu–Tue 9am–6pm), once
home to the Medici and a perfect example of Renaissance
architecture. Inside, the tiny Chapel of the Magi is breathtaking (reservation only tel: (055) 276 0340). Painted by Benozzo
Gozzoli, it depicts the Medici family in the Magi's procession.

Outside cross Via Cavour, go down Via dei Pucci and turn
left at the first intersection, Via Ricasoli, to the **Galleria dell'
Accademia ❶** (Tue–Sun 8.15am–6.50pm; www.accademia.
org), a fine art gallery that contains several transcendent
sculptures by Michelangelo, including his *David*. Michelangelo
completed the statue at the age of 29, and it originally stood
outside the Palazzo Vecchio; it was moved to the Accademia
in 1873. Designed as a public monument, it tends to dwarf
its space here, but remains one of the most popular sights in
the city. The hall leading to *David* contains *The Slaves*, which
Michelangelo began some 20 years later. The figures appear to
be unfinished, and the artist's intention is a subject of debate
among art historians. Whatever the case, this work seems to
typify Michelangelo's belief that sculpture is an 'art that takes
away superfluous material'.

A few steps further up Via Ricasoli are the church and monastery of **San Marco** (Mon–Fri 8.15am–1.50pm, Sat–Sun until 4.50pm, closed 2nd and 4th Mon, 1st, 3rd and 5th Sun of the month). A monastery has stood here since medieval times; in 1437 it was converted into a Dominican retreat by Cosimo de' Medici, and soon became the site of Europe's first public library. One of the early friars was the artist Fra Angelico, and the monastery was also the home of Savonarola, the puritanical preacher, who was prior here before being burned at the stake in 1498. The museum, entered off a cloister, has many of Fra Angelico's devotional images, painted with loving detail, but his masterpieces are in the Dormitory, where the monks lived. They include the *Annunciation*, at the top of the stairs, and others in various rooms, designed to inspire the monks in their contemplations.

Ponte Vecchio, the only bridge that survived World War II

ACROSS THE PONTE VECCHIO TO THE OLTRARNO

The traditional way to cross the River Arno is on foot, via the **Ponte Vecchio** ❶. It was built in 1345, on the site of an older wooden bridge, and is the only one of the city's bridges that wasn't mined by the German army during World War II. Its stalls are lined with shops, many selling jewellery. Via Guicciardini leads directly to the **Palazzo Pitti** ❻ (www.uffizi.it), an immense structure begun in the middle of the 15th century to a design by Brunelleschi; the original Renaissance concept is now almost completely obscured by additions made over the next few centuries. The Pitti family were rivals in wealth and power to the Medicis; the palace was intended as a statement to that effect. As fate would have it, the Medicis eventually moved into the Pitti Palace themselves.

The palace contains four museums, most notably the **Galleria Palatina** (Tue–Sun 8.15am–6.50pm), a series of ornately decorated

⊘ MICHELANGELO

After proving his ability in the workshop of Domenico Ghirlandaio, Michelangelo (1475–1564) was sent at just 14 years of age to serve in the court of Florence's most important patron, Lorenzo de' Medici. The artist was still a young man when he secured his reputation with the *Pietà* in St Peter's in Rome. He was to return there to work on the ceiling of the Sistine Chapel, but not before he enriched Florence with such works as *David*, now in the Galleria dell'Accademia. Michelangelo's sculptures can be found throughout Florence, in the Medici Chapels, the Museo dell'Opera del Duomo, the Casa Buonarotti (a museum dedicated to Michelangelo, located at Via Ghibellina 70), the Bargello and Palazzo Vecchio, to name just a few.

apartments that house an excellent collection of High Renaissance art. In the Sala di Apollo are two works by Titian – his *Portrait of an Unknown Gentleman* and a golden portrayal of *Mary Magdalene*. The Sala di Giove contains Raphael's *La Velata*, a serene portrait of his Roman mistress. Raphael also fills the Sala di Saturno, particularly his *Madonna della Seggiola*, a rounded depiction that seems to curve off the can-

Statue in Boboli Gardens

vas. Other museums in the complex include one devoted to modern art, one to decorative arts, and one to costume and fashion.

Directly behind Pitti Palace, the lovely **Giardini di Boboli** (Boboli Gardens; daily 8.15am–sunset, closed 1st and last Mon of the month) have been open to the public since 1766. The paths traverse a steep hill, beautifully planted and with many shady corners. In an amphitheatre in the centre, the Medicis staged lavish entertainments that involved singing and dancing and were probably an early form of opera. The gardens are dotted with sculpture; note especially the Grotto del Buontalenti to the left of the entrance, a man-made cave complete with stalactites, stone animals and copies of Michelangelo's famous statues *The Slaves*. The originals stood here until 1909 and are now in the Galleria dell' Accademia (see page 40). The Forte di Belvedere, at the crest of the hill, provides a wonderful view of the city, with the Duomo floating above the skyline.

From the Palazzo Pitti, the **Oltrarno** neighbourhood extends both east and west along the Arno. Heading west, you'll find tiny streets that open onto the piazza and church of **Santo Spirito** (Mon, Tue, Thu–Sat 10am–12.30pm, Sun 4–5.30pm; free), which, with its unadorned facade, is another good example of Brunelleschi's Renaissance architecture. Continuing on, **Santa Maria del Carmine** (Mon and Wed–Sat 10am–5pm, Sun 1–5pm) houses Tuscan artist Masaccio's masterful Brancacci Chapel, painted in the 1420s.

Eastbound along the river, you will eventually come to the Porta San Niccolò, an original piece of the city walls, where you can start a climb to **Piazzale Michelangelo**. Ascending the ramps behind San Niccolò, you eventually come to the piazza with the most acclaimed panoramic view of Florence. Home to the second replica of the *David*, the piazza offers a commanding vista of the city, and many Florentines and tourists gather here for the sunset.

From Piazzale Michelangelo, you can take the road further up the hill towards the Romanesque-style church of **San Miniato al Monte** ❶ (Mon–Sat 9.30am–1pm, 3–7/8pm, Sun 8.15am–7pm; free). This church, with a still working monastery, is renowned for its *Christ between the Virgin and St Minias* mosaic, dating back to the mid-13th century.

AROUND FLORENCE

While Florence itself can be all-consuming, several spots nearby provide delightful day trips, and an opportunity to get a different perspective on the city itself.

FIESOLE

Fiesole ❷, perched on the hills to the northeast 8km (5 miles) from Florence, is one such town. (Take the No. 7 ATAF bus

The hills of Fiesole

from Santa Maria Novella station.) Originally settled by the Etruscans, the municipality waged an uneasy battle with its larger, richer neighbour for centuries – until 1125, when the Florentines attacked and levelled it, piously preserving only the cathedral and the bishop's palace. Since then, Fiesole has been a retreat for the city's wealthy from the summer heat and humidity, a heritage that shows today in its many beautifully kept villas, each surrounded by extensive gardens.

Fiesole's centre is the **Piazza Mino**, a fine spot for an iced drink on a hot day; from here you can admire the **Duomo** and its graceful campanile. Via Marini, off the piazza, leads to the Area Archeologica (Mar–Oct daily 10am–6/7pm, Nov–Feb Wed–Mon 10am–3pm; www.museidifiesole.it) where you will find a **Roman theatre**. The 3,000-seat theatre, built in the 1st century BC, was excavated at the end of the 19th; it is well preserved and still used for performances. Three arches nearby

Villa Medici, just outside Fiesole

mark the site of the Roman baths, and from here it is possible to view a stretch of the original Etruscan city walls. Signs to the east of the theatre point up a hill towards three **Etruscan tombs** dating from the 3rd century BC.

You might wish to walk back to Florence on the signposted old Fiesole road; if so, stop on the way to admire the gardens of the **Villa Medici**, which are open to the public (8.15am–dusk, but check ahead as opening times are limited in winter; tel: (055) 452 691).

THE MUGELLO

A few kilometres north of Florence, the Apennine foothills and the Sieve river basin form the **Mugello** region, which is characterised by gentle hills and fertile valleys, olive groves, vineyards, oak and chestnut woods. (It can be reached by bus from Florence or by car from the Barberino di Mugello exit of the A1.)

The Mugello has great associations with the Medici, the Italian Renaissance's most important family, who originated from here and built many of their extravagant villas around the countryside. At first these country houses were fortified hideouts, but in more peaceful times they became luxurious second (or third) homes.

The restored **Villa Cafaggiolo** (closed for restoration), originally a fortress, was altered in 1451 by architect Michelozzo at the request of Cosimo de' Medici to create a country retreat where writers and artists were lavishly entertained. A little further south, **Castello del Trebbio** received similar treatment at the hands of Michelozzo and, more than any other 15th-century Tuscan villa, retains the feudal atmosphere of Medici times. The castle is open for guided tours that take in the olive groves and wine tasting (to book tel: (055) 830 4900).

CHIANTI

South of Florence is the lovely **Chianti** country, an area of clustered peaks surrounded by rolling hills and crossed by a multitude of streams. Grapes have been planted and fermented in this temperate, rural region for thousands of years, and despite recent immigration by more northerly Europeans who summer and retire here, it has maintained a sense of peace and purpose.

Although most major towns are served by train and/or bus from Florence and Siena (the cities are 70km/43 miles apart), the best way to appreciate Chianti is by car. Although you can speed through the region in about half an hour on a modern motorway that links the two towns, the best route to take is the SR222, the **Chiantigiana**, which winds through the heart of the region in leisurely fashion and links to the myriad of tiny roads that serve it.

It can be difficult to find the start of the SR222, but you really don't want to settle for one of the alternative, less attractive routes to Siena; from central Florence, look for the Firenze

Certosa or Firenze Sud entrances to the A1 *autostrada*, which speeds south to Rome; the Chiantigiana and the first village you come to on the road, Grassina, are well signposted from either entrance. You'll need a good map and a sense of adventure because, while many of the loveliest towns and most famous vineyards are near the motorway, the most rewarding stops are those you will discover yourself.

Arguably the bestrecognised wine in the world, Chianti was created by the Grand Duke Cosimo de' Medici III in 1716, when he declared that only certain parts of Tuscany could call their wine Chianti.

Drive slowly south to **Greve ❸**, 45km (28 miles) from Florence, the centre of the wine trade and the host each September of the region's largest wine fair. Greve began life as a market town

The famous Chianti bottle

in the 13th or 14th century and has slowly grown to become Chianti's unofficial capital. Its charming central **Piazza Matteotti** is lined with a patchwork of arcades, each built by a different wine-grower. The statue in the centre of the square is of Giovanni Verrazano, the European discoverer of New York harbour, who was born nearby. You will notice that there is a wine shop on nearly every corner, many offering tastings, and all stocking varieties unavailable elsewhere.

Greve's castle burned down in the 14th century, and its former convent houses a museum of sacred art (Thu–Fri 10am–1pm, Sat–Sun 4–8pm, shorter hours in winter). But just 1km (0.5mile) to the west is the castle of **Montefioralle**, a well-restored fortification

Wine-tasting

Many vineyards give tours of their wine cellars and arrange special tastings, usually for a minimal price. This is a great opportunity to take part in the local wine-producing tradition.

with octagonal walls and two fine Romanesque churches. It provides an evocative image of the region as it once was.

Radda, some 10km (6 miles) south of Greve, has a lovely and well-preserved historic centre, and is an appealing spot for a stroll. On the way there, you might wish to make a short detour to the **Castello di Volpaia**, one of the region's wine estates that has developed into a small tourist town offering tours, tastings and products for sale. Most of the large medieval castle is gone now, but the central keep still stands. The surrounding village is medieval in tone but contains a pretty Renaissance church. Just east of Radda is the **Badia a Coltibuono**, an abbey founded in 770, now an agricultural estate that produces a fine red wine.

THE ROAD TO LUCCA

Heading west from Florence the road to Lucca passes through changing terrain, as well as several fascinating towns that are well worth visiting in their own right.

PRATO

Prato lies 17km (10 miles) to the northwest of Florence. The 15th-century **Duomo**, in the central piazza, is fronted by an

Andrea della Robbia terracotta over the portal, and the Pulpit of the Sacred Girdle, with friezes by Donatello (originals are now in the museum), on the southwest corner. Inside the Duomo, frescoes by Filippo Lippi surround the altar.

On the southern outskirts of Prato you'll find the **Villa Medici di Poggio a Caiano** ❹ (daily 8.15am–6.30pm, with exceptions; free; reservations required for museum tel: (055) 877 012), one of the earliest and most typical Medici villas. Lorenzo the Magnificent bought a farmhouse on the site in 1480, then had it rebuilt in the Renaissance style. It is raised on a podium; the entrance is actually through the basement, which is furnished with games rooms and a private theatre. Upstairs is a huge salon, decorated with lovely frescoes, and the gardens are a pleasant place to stroll. On the second floor is the Museum of Still Life.

PISTOIA

Pistoia ❺, 35km (21 miles) northwest of Florence (accessible by train or bus; by car, take the A11 or SR435), has a medieval centre with narrow alleys. Pistoia was the seat of battles that plagued Tuscany in the 13th century and, appropriately, its name is the

---

⊙ VIA FRANCIGENA

Many Tuscan towns witnessed an increase in activity and a jump in population during medieval pilgrimages to Rome along the Via Francigena, a route roughly 1,600km (1,000 miles) long that led from Canterbury in southern England all the way to Rome. At the end of the 10th century the Archbishop of Canterbury documented his trip along this road from England through France to Switzerland, then through Tuscany, including stops in Lucca, San Gimignano and Siena, and finally to Rome.

Piazza Anfiteatro, Lucca

origin of the word 'pistol'. Today it is a busy industrial city, and the site of some lovely Romanesque churches. The **Duomo** (daily 8am–12.30pm, 4–7pm), in the central piazza, was built in the 13th century and contains the remarkable **Chapel of San Jacopo**, a construction of gilded silver decorated with medieval saints and scenes from the Bible. Two prophets, carved by Brunelleschi, stand on the right. The **Ospedale del Ceppo** is a hospital founded in the 13th century that was still in use until 2013. The terracottas on the facade illustrate the cardinal and theological virtues, depicted by Giovanni della Robbia (son of Andrea).

MONTECATINI TERME

Just west of Pistoia is Valdinievole, or the Valley of the Mists, where spas are fed by underground springs and Florentines have for centuries sought a cure for the excesses of city life. The best-known is **Montecatini Terme**, 46km (28 miles) west of Florence and 12km (7 miles) west of Pistoia (easily reached by train from either, or by car via the A11 or SR435). Here the waters are sulphurous and the shopping luxurious. The centre of town is the **Parco dei Termi**, where a row of spas housed in neoclassical temples perch over various springs. Most are open for mud wraps, mineral elixirs and relaxation every day year-round.

LUCCA

A graceful and prosperous provincial capital, 77km (47 miles) west of Florence on the A11, **Lucca** ❻ is encased by peculiarly elegant 16th-century walls – protective as well as decorative. The city is less visited than some surrounding spots, yet has a considerable charm, along with some famous musical sons, Boccherini and Puccini among them. To get a sense of the city, take a stroll or a bicycle ride along the tops of the walls, which are planted with plane trees and provide lovely views; note the grid layout of the streets, a remnant of the city's Roman past. You might also note a paucity of cars. More than other Italians, Luccans tend to ride bicycles, and this makes the city a bit more pedestrian-friendly than most in Italy.

The **Cattedrale di San Martino** (Mon–Fri 9.30am–6pm, Sat 9.30am–6.45pm, Sun noon–6pm), on the piazza of the same name, has an asymmetric facade of green and white marble decorated with a striking assortment of little columns. Note the pillar next to the tower; it is carved with a 12th-century labyrinth, a symbol of just how hard it is to get to Heaven. Under it are 13th-century stone reliefs; the sculptures around the doors are by Nicola Pisano and others. Inside, in the sacristy, is the moving tomb of Ilaria Carretto Guinigi. Made by Jacopo della Quercia in the 15th century, it commemorates the young wife of a rich Luccan, memorialising her beauty. The octagonal Tempietto

(Little Temple) by Matteo Civitali was built to house the Volto Santo, a wooden statue of Jesus crucified that is said to have been carved by Nicodemus. The museum across the street from the Cathedral contains the gold and jewel-encrusted ornaments used to dress the Volto Santo on special holidays.

A few blocks away, on the Piazza San Michele, is **San Michele in Foro** (daily 7.40am–noon, 3–6pm), a

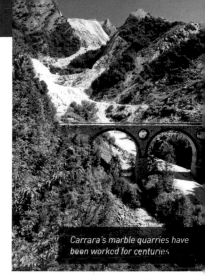

Carrara's marble quarries have been worked for centuries

12th-century Romanesque church with a lovely facade. The body of the church is unfinished, and so the facade, with its rows of columns, each one different from the other, towers above it with the upper levels fronting pure air. The effect is magical. Inside, in the right nave, is an ornately painted organ and a painting by Filippino Lippi of various saints. Opera-lovers may wish to visit the church of **Paolino**, just two blocks to the west, where Puccini was once the organist.

THE GARFAGNANA

North of the lowlands around Lucca are dramatic snow-capped mountains, terraced hillsides, deep gorges and mountain streams, populated by deer, wild boar, badgers and wolves, not to mention flocks of walkers, canoeists, rock climbers and cavers. This area, known as the **Garfagnana**, is packed with scenic routes and protected nature reserves.

Of great importance is the marble quarry town of **Carrara** ❼ accessible by car from the A12, which connects to the A11 out of Lucca. There are extraordinary views down into the quarries, which have supplied sculptors with raw material for centuries.

PISA AND THE COAST

The Tuscan coast is a land apart from the rest of the province, separated from the valleys of central Tuscany by a coastal ridge of the Apennines and so different in appearance you won't associate it with any of the familiar images of vineyard-clad hills and undulating valleys. Here the landscape is flat, even marshy in parts, and often punctuated with oil refineries, cranes, bustling ports, and other accessories of the business of modern life. This is not to say there are not places that reward your journey to this part of Tuscany. Pisa is here, and Livorno offers the chance to explore a working port city and enjoy a seafood meal.

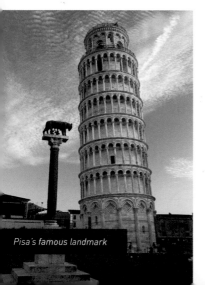
Pisa's famous landmark

PISA

The university town of **Pisa** ❽, 25km (16 miles) southwest of Lucca, was a maritime power in the 11th century and one of the largest and most cosmopolitan cities in Europe; its lovely centre is a testament to those days. From Lucca, take route SS12 or the A11 and A12 *autostrade* to Pisa; there are also frequent bus and train services between Lucca and Pisa. If you plan to make a day trip to Pisa directly from Florence (the distance is 77km/47 miles), take the A11 and A12 *autostrade*.

By the 14th century, Pisa's harbour had silted over, and the city, like much of Tuscany, had fallen under the hegemony of the Florentines. Over the centuries, Pisa's most notable achievements have

The Leaning Tower

The tower leans at an angle of 3.97 degrees. Its height is 55.86m (183ft) from the ground on the lower side and 56.7m (186ft) on the higher side, making the top 3.9 metres (13ft) from the vertical. There are 296 or 294 steps; the seventh floor has two fewer steps on the north-facing staircase. The thickness of the walls at the base is 4.1m (13.5ft) and at the top 2.5m (8ft). The tower's weight is estimated at 14,500 metric tonnes.

been intellectual – it is the seat of a university, home to Galileo and, in more recent times, the physicist Enrico Fermi. Thousands of tourists flock here, however, to see one famous landmark – the Leaning Tower, which is located, together with the Baptistery and the Duomo, on one of the loveliest squares in the world, the wide grassy expanse of the **Campo dei Miracoli**.

Thanks to its unstable subsoil, the **Leaning Tower** (Campanile; daily, Apr–Aug 8.30am–10pm, Sept–Oct 9am–8pm, Nov–Mar 9am–6pm) has always tilted. Begun in 1173, it began to lean when only three of its eight storeys had been completed. The overhang increased over time, and by the late 20th century it was 4.4m (15ft) out of alignment. Fearing an imminent collapse, the authorities closed the tower in 1990 while engineers sought a remedy. It was finally decided that soil should be extracted from the foundations on the opposite side to the lean, and by 2001 the top of the tower had been brought back 45cm. The tower is open to the public once more, with 30 people allowed up the 251 steps at a time (guided tours every 35 minutes; book in advance to avoid disappointment: www.opapisa.it).

The 12th-century tower isn't the only crooked building on the square; its contemporary, the **Baptistery** (daily, Apr–Oct 8am–8pm, Nov–Mar 9am–6pm), tilts slightly to the north. The largest in Italy, the Baptistery's lower parts are Romanesque, while the upper levels were decorated in Gothic style by sculptors Nicola and Giovanni Pisano; the originals are now in the Museo dell'Opera del Duomo. The interior is strikingly bare, with fine acoustics.

The **Duomo** (daily, Mar–Sept 10am–8pm, Oct 10am–7pm, Nov–Feb 10am–6pm), started in the 11th century, is a lovely example of Pisan Romanesque, with its colonnaded exterior subtly patterned in grey and white stone. The Portale di San Ranieri, an original bronze doorway, is still in place. Cast by Bonnano Pisano in the 12th century, it shows scenes from the life of Christ. The interior, remodelled after a 16th-century fire, is mostly Renaissance. A fine pulpit by Giovanni Pisano survived the fire, however, and the figures on its densely carved surface seem to be rising freely from the base. Note the bronze chandelier near the pulpit – legend has it that Galileo devised his laws regarding the movement of pendulums while watching it (or a predecessor) swing during mass one morning.

The 13th-century cemetery, the **Camposanto** (same hours as the Baptistery) at the north end of the Campo dei Miracoli, was built to hold the soil a local archbishop carried back from Golgotha, so that Pisans might be buried in holy earth. It has an unearthly beauty today, constructed in the shape of a huge cloister, with tombs of many styles and ages lining its arcades.

The **Museo dell'Opera del Duomo** (re-opening early 2019), also on the Piazza, contains many statues and other works from the Duomo and Baptistery.

THE VERSILIA

The flat, pine-covered landscape along the Pisan coast has historically attracted the attention of scholars, poets, writers and artists. Today, the **Versilia** is a popular holiday spot for Italians and others, who spend the hot summer days near the sea in **Viareggio**, a town made famous by its grand *carnevale* celebration and lively boardwalk; or in the seaside retreats around the **Lake of Massaciuccoli**. (From Lucca take the A11 west; from Pisa take the SS1 north.)

LIVORNO

The busy port city of **Livorno** ❾, known to most English-speakers as Leghorn), 19km (12 miles) south of Pisa on the SS1 or A12, has an appealing, working-class aura and, for the sight-weary traveller, a refreshing lack of famous churches. It is chiefly known for two things: the sculptor and painter Amadeo Modigliani was born here in 1884; and the city's seafood restaurants are among the best in Italy.

The Versilia awaits visitors

Originally a Roman port, Livorno reached prominence when Pisa's harbour began to silt up. Under the Medici it became a free port, and a group of refugees including Jews, Greeks, Muslims and Roman Catholics from England took up residence here, making it one of the most cosmopolitan cities of the Renaissance. In World War II it was heavily bombed; since then, it has thrived on the container shipping trade. The original Medici port included a series of canals that have inspired some to call Livorno a little Venice. The best place to see the original plan is the **Porto Mediceo** on the water. The **Duomo** (daily 9am–noon, 5–7pm) in the Piazza Grande has a doorway designed by Inigo Jones, who based his plan for London's Covent Garden on this square.

ELBA

It's impossible, when in Tuscany, not to think of the best-known Napoleonic palindrome in the English language – able was I ere I saw Elba – and it's equally difficult to resist the place itself. One of Italy's largest islands, **Elba ⑩**, which can be reached by ferry from Piombino, has fine beaches, clear water for swimming and mountains ideal for hiking.

The chief town, **Portoferraio**, has a charming old section fortified under the Medici; enter it through the Porta al Mare. In the upper section is **Palazzina dei Mulini** (Mon, Wed–Sat 8.30am–7pm, Sun 8.30am–1pm), where Napoleon lived during his nine-month exile here. Together with his

Tuscan archipelago

Elba is actually part of a group of seven islands that make up the Tuscan Archipelago. Others include Gilgio, the second-biggest and a popular spot for family holidays, which can be reached from Porto Santo Stefano, and tiny Capraia, which can be reached from Livorno.

second home, Villa San Martino, a short drive south of Portoferraio, it is now a National Museum.

A good network of roads traverses the island, and while most spots are served by local buses, mopeds are available for rent and probably provide the best means of exploring. While there are fine beaches everywhere, some of the best are on the south coast, especially at **Marina di Campo**. In the eastern part

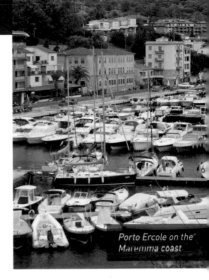
Porto Ercole on the Maremma coast

of the island, **Rio nell'Elba** is the former mining centre; there's a museum of mining at its port, Rio Marina, with a display of local minerals. The town of **Poggio**, in the west, is in a lush area and serves as a starting point for some lovely hikes.

THE MAREMMA

South of Livorno, the **Parco Naturale della Maremma** ⓫ area, once a mosquito-infested swampland but now transformed, has over 100km (60 miles) of coastline, as well as Etruscan sites, medieval villages, hills, valleys and woods. Many of the beaches are in colourful resorts where you pay for entrance and a deck-chair. The marshy inland area has become one of Tuscany's hottest spots for wine, and little towns like **Bolgheri** produce some of Italy's priciest bottles. The area also has mountain villages and mining towns like **Sassetta** and **Campiglia Marittima**, which offer an insight into the less touristy areas of Tuscany.

Siena's Il Campo

SIENA AND AROUND

SIENA

Just as Florence is the city of the Renaissance, **Siena** ⓬ belongs to the Middle Ages. Where Florence's greatest attractions are in its museums, Siena's are in its squares and streets, perched on three hills that provide views from many vantage points. To see both Florence and Siena is to appreciate each even more, and no visit to Tuscany should omit either.

Siena was founded by the Etruscans and colonised by the Romans. During its heyday in the 13th and 14th centuries, it was a flourishing centre of trade, banking and art. In May 1348, however, the Black Death reached Siena, severely reducing the population and dealing a blow from which the municipality would never quite recover. Before the epidemic hit, Siena had some

100,000 citizens, but once the disease had run its course only about 30,000 remained. Regional wars and intrigue followed, until a siege by the Medicis in the 16th century devastated the city, reducing it to an insignificant part of the Florentine Empire. Those events have, in a sense, frozen Siena in time, and the city remains very much as it was in the 14th century.

Il Campo

The heart of the city, the **Piazza del Campo** Ⓐ, known as **Il Campo**, is situated at the intersection of the three ridges upon which Siena sprawls. Laid out in the mid-14th century, the nine paved divisions of the fan-shaped piazza represent the Council of Nine, which governed the medieval city. The **Palazzo Pubblico** Ⓓ, Siena's town hall since 1310, stands on the east side – a fine example of Gothic architecture, topped by the graceful **Torre del Mangia** (Mar–mid–Oct 10am–7pm, mid–Oct–Feb 10am–4pm). If you can manage the 500 or so steps to the top, the tower provides a stunning view of the city.

In the town hall is Siena's **Museo Civico** (daily mid-Mar–Oct 10am–7pm, Nov–mid-Mar 10am–6pm), set in a series of formal state rooms on the upper floors. The Sala del Mappamondo contains some wonderful frescoes by Simone Martini. Note especially his *Maestà*, a beautifully coloured, richly decorative depiction of the *Virgin Enthroned* that is his first known work, painted when he was 30 years old.

City connections

Siena is well connected to Florence by the Tiemme bus company (www.tiemmespa.it), which runs about once an hour Monday to Saturday, and less frequently on Sunday. Take the rapid line (131R), which is non-stop and takes about an hour and 15 minutes.

The facade of Siena's Duomo

In the Sala dei Nove is Ambrogio Lorenzetti's *Allegory of Good and Bad Government*, one of the most important secular works of medieval Europe. The city shown is Siena, quite recognisable even today, and in the artist's allegorical scheme, good government, wearing the colours of a Sienese leader, is surrounded by the virtues, while bad government, ruled by fear, is surrounded by representations of the vices.

The Duomo and Art Gallery

Siena's **Duomo** ⊙ (www.operaduomo.siena.it), a few minutes' walk south of Il Campo, is, in a sense, another victim of the Black Death. While it was initially completed in 1215, a new nave was started in the 14th century but was abandoned when the plague struck. It still stands, unfinished. The original structure, however, is lovely. The facade, designed by Giovanni Pisano, is boldly patterned in black and white marble, and this pattern is repeated in the interior's pavement, which also contains dozens of inlaid panels created by local artists. The pulpit in the left aisle, the work of Nicola Pisano, is carved with panels depicting the life of Christ; supporting columns rest on stone lions.

The **Museo dell'Opera Metropolitana** (daily, Mar–Oct 10.30am–7pm, Nov–Feb until 5.30pm; www.operaduomo. siena.it), housed in the cathedral's unfinished nave, contains most of the original facade statuary, as well as a magnificent altarpiece by Duccio. Painted in the early 14th century, it is a majestic example of late medieval art, and the central figure of the Virgin is a study in serenity. The Treasury Room upstairs contains a gilded silver reliquary; a staircase leads to a walkway that provides a wonderful view.

Across from the Duomo is **Santa Maria della Scala** (mid-Oct–mid-Mar 10am–5pm, rest of year until 7pm, with exceptions; www.santamariadellascala.com), one of the oldest

◉ THE PALIO

On 2 July and 16 August each year, Siena is cheerfully and noisily disturbed by the Palio, a more or less free-for-all horse race around the Campo. The Palio has its roots in the old divisions of the city, whereby Siena was divided into *contrade*, or neighbourhood wards, which served as small political units, each with its own governing body, social club and local parish. The number of *contrade* was fixed at 17 in 1675; of these, 10 can sponsor horses that run in the two annual Palio races. The theory of the race is based on chance – the *contrade* draw their horse and starting position by lot.

The race consists of three laps around the Campo on a sanded and well-padded course. The winner is the horse, mounted or not, that completes the circuit first. The single rule of the race is that jockeys may not interfere with each other's reins. Needless to say, mayhem ensues.

As this race stirs enormous passions, seats are impossible to come by unless you book well in advance. Your best bet is to appear in the square well before starting time and mark out your spot.

hospitals in Europe. Today it is a huge museum and exhibition complex displaying important artwork. Transferred from its original home on Via della Sapienza, the Museo Archeologico's collection is displayed here along impressive tuff tunnels.

Just a bit further south is Siena's art gallery, the **Pinacoteca Nazionale** Ⓔ (Tue–Sat 8.15am–7.15pm Mon and Sun 9am–1pm), housed in a 14th-century palace. The works on display range from the 12th century to the Renaissance. Note especially Guido da Siena's *Scenes from the Life of Christ*, one of the first known paintings on canvas; Simone Martini's *Madonna and Child*; and Beccafumi's cartoons for the floor panels in the Duomo.

VAL D'ELSA

A number of surprisingly pastoral hill towns are perched to the north and west of Siena in the **Val d'Elsa** region. They are an easy and scenic drive from the city, and the public bus service from Siena will also take you there. As you travel through the area, you may well be overcome by the feeling that you've experienced this landscape before. You have, in a sense, because the rolling hills – a reddish-brown colour (known appropriately as burned siena) in places where the soil has been tilled, forested in part with cypress and pine, and often crowned by medieval cities – form the background of many Renaissance paintings.

The best way to explore these towns is to immerse yourself in the Tuscan countryside by making the scenic drive from Florence through Chianti country on route SR222 to Siena (see page 47), then approaching them from that lovely city. If, however, you are making the trip directly from Florence, you can bypass Siena by taking the speedy RA3 south to Monteriggioni, a trip of 55km (33 miles), and begin your explorations there.

Monteriggioni ⑬, 15km (9 miles) northwest of Siena on the RA3, once provided the Sienese with a lookout point for Florentine

The towers and fortified walls of Monteriggioni

troops, and its 14 towers and fortified walls still stand, perhaps the best-preserved in Italy. They protect a tiny town within that is not much larger than a football pitch. Construction on this bastion started in the early 13th century and, girded by stone as it is, the village hasn't grown much since. Dante likened the towers to a circle of Titans guarding the lowest level of hell and his verse, from the *Inferno*, faces you as you enter Monteriggioni. There are some houses and a few restaurants inside the walls, but not much to do except soak up the charm of the place.

Colle di Val d'Elsa, about 10km (6 miles) further along the RA3 and the SR68 (simply follow the road signs, which often do not indicate route numbers), must be approached from the correct angle. The lower town, which you will see first if you enter from the east, consists of unlovely housing tracts and factories. Enter instead from the west, and you will pass under a 16th-century gate into the Old Town.

Medieval San Gimignano

Via del Castello, the main street, stretches along a ridge, and is lined with medieval houses. Arnolfo di Cambio, architect of Florence's Duomo, was born at No. 63. The street leads on to the **Piazza del Duomo** and the Cathedral. Originally a Romanesque structure, the Cathedral was rebuilt in the 17th and 18th centuries. Inside, however, is a fine marble 15th-century pulpit, a lovely *Nativity* by Rutilio Manetti and, commanding pride of place, the Cappella del Santo Chiodo, which contains a nail said to come from the True Cross. Just off the piazza is the 16th-century **Palazzo Campana**, a Mannerist-style mansion.

SAN GIMIGNANO

Around 11km (7 miles) north of Colle di Val d'Elsa, **San Gimignano 14** presents a stunning skyline, with its tall, beautifully preserved medieval towers. Inside the walls, the town's lovely streets and churches, its medieval and rural atmosphere, and its fine collections of art have made it a popular destination for tourists – too popular, perhaps, because in season it fills up with day-trippers, and its chief industry seems to be the selling of postcards. But out of season, or in the evenings when many visitors have departed, the town provides everything its other-worldly beauty promises.

Founded by the Etruscans, San Gimignano was named in the 5th century to honour a bishop of Modena who reputedly saved the village from Attila the Hun. It prospered during the Middle Ages, then was struck hard by the Black Death, and entered the modern era as a desperately poor backwater. Tourism has changed all that, and the town now prospers because of its beauty and a fine local white wine called Vernaccia.

At its heart is the Piazza del Duomo and the **Collegiata or Duomo** (Apr–Oct Mon–Fri 10am–7pm, Sat 10am–5.30pm, Sun 12.30–7.30pm, Nov–Jan and Mar Mon–Sat 10am–5pm, Sun 12.30–5pm; www.duomosangimignano.it), the town's largest church. The foundations of the church were laid in the 11th century; much of what you see now was constructed in the 15th. The interior is grandly decorated with frescoes. Note especially the New Testament scenes on the right-hand wall painted by Lippo Memmi in the 14th century. The Cappella di Santa Fina, off the right aisle, was built in the 15th century by Giuliano de Maiano. The frescoes, by Domenico Ghirlandaio, depict the life of Santa Fina, a local girl who attained sainthood status for her piety. The **Torre Grossa** (Apr–Sept 10am–7.30pm, Oct–Mar 11am–5.30pm; entry only with a combined ticket to the complex of the Civic Museums; www.sangimignanomusei.it), also on the piazza, is the tallest of the town's towers at 54m (175ft). It dates from the early 14th century, and provides an extraordinary view of the surrounding Tuscan countryside. The adjacent **Piazza della Cisterna** is ringed by cafés, restaurants and *gelaterie*.

VOLTERRA

Some 37km (23 miles) west on a lovely drive through undulating farm country interspersed now and then with vineyards, orchards, and little copses (from San Gimignano, drop south to route SR68) is **Volterra** ⑮, a lofty town stretched along a high ridge and home to a wonderful collection of Etruscan art. The ancient city, in the centre of a rich mining region, was much larger than what remains today. Settled first by the Etruscans, then, centuries later, taken by the Florentines in a bloody siege, it is now a quiet and somewhat mysterious place.

The heart of Volterra is the **Piazza dei Priori**, which is almost entirely surrounded by medieval buildings. The 13th-century **Palazzo dei Priori** probably served as the model for Florence's Palazzo Vecchio, and its tower provides an excellent view. The **Palazzo Vescovile** (Bishop's Palace), also on the piazza, houses a small museum containing a bust of St Linus by Andrea della Robbia. The 12th-century **Duomo** is just off the square; it has a wonderful ceiling, carved and decorated with gold and azure. Note also the *Crucifixion*, a fine example of Baroque work, painted by Francesco Curradi in 1611. The **Pinacoteca e Museo Civico** (mid-Mar–Oct daily 10.30am–5.30pm, Nov–mid-Mar Sat–Sun 10am–4.30pm; www.museivaldicecina.it), also off the piazza, has some fine pieces by local artists, notably Rosso Fiorentino's *Descent from the Cross*.

The real reason most people come to Volterra is to see what the Etruscans left. The **Museo Etrusco Guarnacci**, on Via Don Minzoni, houses a large collection of Etruscan artefacts, most found in the area (mid-Mar–Oct daily 10.30am–5.30pm, Nov–mid-Mar Sat–Sun 10am–4.30pm; www.museivaldicecina.it). Most notable are its funerary urns, a few of which date from the 9th century BC. The urns, in the form of rectangular boxes, are carved with striking depictions of the deceased; many show touching farewells, and together the 600 or so urns provide a fascinating picture of Etruscan beliefs about death and, by extension, life. Note especially the *Gli Sposi* (the Married Couple), a 1st-century BC urn decorated with the faces of an elderly couple, as penetrating and passionate-looking now as

Monte Oliveto Maggiore

they must have been in life, some 2,000 years ago. The museum also contains some bronzes; note especially the *Ombra della Sera* (the Shadow of the Night), a delicate and elongated nude.

The **Balze**, as Volterra's eroded cliffs are called, are a short walk northwest of the piazza along Via di San Lino. Here time and the weather are eating away the edge of the city, and the walls are literally dropping into chasms. Ancient alabaster mines gouge into the cliffs; below them are huge buried tracts of the original Etruscan settlement.

SOUTHERN TUSCANY

Southern Tuscany summons up superlatives like enchanting, bucolic, magical – and this is no exaggerated praise. If, in your mind, you can superimpose these words on a landscape shaped by vineyards, solitary farmhouses and medieval castles, you'll have a good idea of what awaits you. This region is best explored by car, which gives you the freedom to appreciate the marvellous rural vistas.

MONTE OLIVETO MAGGIORE

The area just south of Siena is a primeval landscape of stark beauty. Appropriately called **Le Crete**, it is a moonscape of interlocking pale-clay hummocks, stands of cypress trees and barren gullies, rich in wildlife and loved by Sienese city dwellers. **Monte Oliveto Maggiore** ⓰ (daily 9.15am–noon, 3.15–5pm; free; www.monte-oliveto.it), around 30km (20 miles) south of Siena, is set here (follow the SR2 towards the town of Buonconvento, and from there the SS451 to Monte Oliveto). The monastery, reached through a gatehouse adorned with terracottas by the 15th-century Florentine sculptor Luca della Robbia, was founded around 1200 by a Sienese man who, after going blind, took the name Bernardo and came here with two companions to live a solitary life. He attracted followers, and the group was soon recognised by the Church as the Olivetans – otherwise known as the white Benedictines. Over the next few centuries, the monastery became one of the most eminent in Italy, home to a remarkable series of frescoes showing the life of St Benedict. Started by Luca Signorelli in the late 15th century and finished by Il Sodoma in the 16th, they are in the great cloister of the monastery, and well worth a careful perusal.

MONTALCINO

Montalcino, just off the SR2 further south, is set on a hill under the silhouette of a perfectly preserved castle, and from a distance this walled town presents a magical sight. Its fortunes have swung wildly throughout history. An ally of Siena (which is just 53km/32 miles to the north), it became the last bastion of the republic in 1555, when for four years a small group of Sienese exiles fought off the Florentines. Succeeding centuries saw the decline of the town into a malariainfested backwater. In the past few decades, however, its fortunes have rebounded, fuelled primarily by the local Brunello wine.

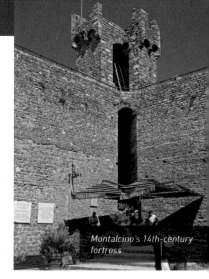

Montalcino's 14th-century fortress

The 14th-century Sienese fortress is less martial these days: inside its walls are a public park, several wine shops and nice restaurants, and its ramparts provide wonderful views. Just down the Via Ricasoli, within the ancient rooms of Sant Agostino's monastery, is the **Museo Civico e Diocesano d'Arte Sacra** (Apr–Dec Tue–Sun 10am–6pm, Jan–Mar 10am–1pm, 2–4pm), one of the most important collects of archaeological, medieval and modern art in the district of Siena. The collection offers an almost complete view of this important Tuscan town's artistic production. The town also has a handful of churches, all of roughly equal interest.

Montalcino has made wine for centuries, but Brunello, developed in the late 19th century, is a relatively recent addition to its output. It has become one of Italy's premier reds, and has turned Montalcino from nearly the poorest to one of the richest towns in Tuscany. Some of the surrounding vineyards – among them Poggio Antico, Banfi and Fattoria dei Barbi – welcome visitors.

PIENZA

Pienza , 20km (12 miles) to the east on the SS146, has one of the oddest pedigrees of any town in Italy. It happened to be the birthplace of 15th-century Pope Pius II, who, upon achieving his eminence, decided to turn the sleepy little village into an ideal Renaissance city. With the help of architect Bernardo Rossellino, he commissioned the construction of a central piazza, cathedral, papal palace and town hall. Unfortunately, Pius ran out of money, so the planned city never grew beyond the central square and its surrounding buildings. They remain, however, as an intact and grand example of planned Renaissance architecture, and nothing else like them exists in Italy.

The **Piazza Pio II**, the central square, is more ideal than real, almost a stage set (it was used as one in Zeffirelli's film *Romeo and Juliet*). The flanking **Duomo** (daily) has a Renaissance facade crowned with the Pope's coat of arms. The interior is Gothic in style; note the five altarpieces painted by artists from Siena, on the theme of the Madonna and Child and the Assumption. The tall windows allow in a flood of light. The **Palazzo Piccolomini** (Tue–Sun 10am–6pm with exceptions, closed 7 Jan–14 Feb and 16–30 Nov), the finest palace on the square, was designed to provide a view, which you can appreciate from the first-floor papal apartments.

Pecorino

Pienza is also well known for its delicious Pecorino cheese. Tiny *alimentari*, or speciality food shops, carry the various types, and many offer cheese-tastings in their stores.

MONTEPULCIANO

The highest of the hill towns, **Montepulciano** is set on a ridge, another 24km (15 miles) to the east of Pienza on the SS146, or 125km (75 miles) south of

Montepulciano is famous for its wine, the Vino Nobile

Florence on the A1 *autostrada*. If you are coming from Cortona, it is a trip of about 35km (21 miles) west across the Valdichiana.

Montepulciano is largely Renaissance in character, and much of what stands today was built by architects from Florence after 1511, when the city joined the Florentine Empire. Its centre is the **Piazza Grande**, placed on the town's highest spot. The **Palazzo Comunale**, on the piazza, is a 14th-century version of Florence's Palazzo Vecchio; its tower (Apr–Oct Mon–Sat 10am–6pm) provides a marvellous view as far as Siena. The 17th-century **Duomo** (daily 9am–noon, 4–6pm), also on the square, has no facade to speak of because the city ran out of money. Its interior is surprisingly elegant, however, and contains two sights of interest. The monumental tomb for papal secretary Bartolomeo Aragazzi, carved in the 15th century by Michelozzo, was taken apart in the 18th century, and pieces are now scattered throughout the church; note the reclining Aragazzi to the right of the central door. And on the high altar is a 15th-century gold triptych by Taddeo di Bartoldo showing the *Assumption of the Virgin*; it is considered his masterpiece.

Another church worth a visit is the 16th-century **Tempio di San Biagio**, designed by Antonio da Sangallo the Elder. Set outside the city walls on the Via San Biagio, it is built of soft travertine and its position allows it to be seen from every side.

Of course, Montepulciano is also known for its wine, the Vino Nobile. Wine has been made here since the 8th century, and the town's shops offer the local variety, along with cheeses and meats to complement it. Some have cellars set in ancient underground tunnels; if they do, ask for a tour.

TUFA TOWNS

Sorano, **Sovana** and **Pitigliano** are three ancient towns carved into the volcanic rock, or tufa, around 60km (40 miles) south of Montepulciano. (They can be reached by driving south on the A1 and then cutting back west.) Their unique placement above dramatic cliffs of soft, porous tufa covered in a jungle of fern, ivy and evergreen trees make them a curious spectacle and a pleasant day trip.

AREZZO AND EASTERN TUSCANY

The landscape of the province of Arezzo is rugged, with steep, thickly wooded valleys that shield its towns and villages from view. To the east of Arezzo are two important towns for Piero della Francesca enthusiasts – Monterchi and Sansepolcro. To the south are the prosperous farms of the fertile Valdichiana, over which the enchanting hill town of Cortona is perched.

AREZZO

The A1 autostrada connects Florence and **Arezzo** , 85km (51 miles) apart, as does the slower but more scenic Strada dei Sette Ponti, so called because the road crosses seven bridges as it winds its way through olive groves and ancient towns.

Arezzo's old centre, girded by well-planned and attractive modern districts, bespeaks the great artistic talent that has flourished here. The **Piazza Grande** is

Arezzo's Piazza Grande

arcaded on one side by a loggia designed by Giorgio Vasari, the 16th-century architect who, enchanting as this assemblage is, will forever be remembered for his accounts of masters more talented than he was, his *Lives of the Artists* – in effect, the first work of art history. Behind the unprepossessing brick facade of the 14th-century **Basilica di San Francesco** (Mon–Fri 9am–5.30pm, Sat 9am–5pm, Sun 1–5pm, longer hours in summer; www.museistataliarezzo.it), just south of the piazza, is a genuinely sublime series of frescoes by Piero della Francesca on the *Legend of the True Cross*. Painted in the 1450s, they show all his skills at perspective and conveying emotion in a restrained way, as well as his feeling for narrative drama.

A few blocks away, on Corso Italia, is **Pieve di Santa Maria**, a 12th-century Romanesque church. Built in cream-coloured stone, its layered arcades narrow as they rise, giving an impression of height; the bell tower 'of the hundred holes' was added later. Above the crypt is a 14th-century polyptych of the *Madonna and Child* by Pietro Lorenzetti.

MONTERCHI AND SANSEPOLCRO

If the San Francesco frescoes have given you a taste for Piero della Francesca's work, you could do no better than to venture northeast to Monterchi and Sansepolcro.

Lago di Trasimeno

The small village of **Monterchi**, just 25km (16 miles) from Arezzo on the SS73, is home to his *Madonna del Parto*, a portrait of the pregnant Madonna, an image rarely seen in Italian art. Originally painted for the local chapel, this solemn yet delicate fresco is now on show at the Museo Madonna del Prato (Wed–Mon 9am–12.30pm, 2–5pm, Apr–Oct until 7pm) in a former primary school on Via Reglia; it is a pilgrimage site for both art-lovers and pregnant women, who come here to pray for an easy birth.

Sansepolcro, another 10km (6 miles) along, was della Francesca's birthplace. It's a quiet town whose main attractions are his *Madonna della Misericordia* and *Resurrection*, in the Museo Civico (daily 10am–1pm, 2.30–6pm; www.museo-civicosansepolcro.it). The *Madonna*, painted around 1440, is the artist's earliest known work; one of the kneeling figures around the Virgin may be a self-portrait. *The Resurrection of Christ*, painted in 1463, is a powerful yet spiritual painting of a muscular Christ emerging from the tomb.

CORTONA AND LAGO DI TRASIMENO

If you travel south of Arezzo for just 30km (18 miles) on the SR71, a busy local road that serves many farming communities and at points is overlooked by little hillside towns and castles, you will come to what is often and justifiably called Tuscany's most beautiful hill town: **Cortona ⓴**.

The Etruscans were among the first to appreciate the lofty heights upon which Cortona is built, and much of what they left behind, including a bronze lamp, is housed in the town's small **Museo dell'Accademia Etrusca** (Apr–Oct daily 10am–7pm, Nov–Mar Tue–Sun until 5pm; www.cortonamaec.org). What is most striking about Cortona, though, belongs to a much later period, and that is its unspoiled medieval architecture. The town is untouched by modern development and unfolds in a series of theatrical piazzas; at its heart, the **Piazza Garibaldi** opens into the **Piazza Signorelli**. The town's other treasures also emerged from the medieval centuries - frescoes and panels by Fra Angelico in the **Museo Diocesano**, across from the Duomo.

One side of Cortona's public gardens opens to a belvedere with sweeping views. Looking south into Umbria you will see a body of water glistening in the distance. This is **Lago di Trasimeno**, Italy's fourth-largest lake. Its shallow waters are very clean and, in summer, full of swimmers, boaters and windsurfers.

INTO UMBRIA

Umbria is a verdant and peaceful region. Its fields and forests roll gently

Heavy defeat

Lake Trasimene might be peaceful now, but in 217BC its waters ran red with the blood of Roman legions, more than 16,000 of whom were slaughtered by Hannibal's troops in one of Rome's worst defeats.

across the central Italian landscape, and when viewed from the belvederes of the proud medieval hill towns the land seems to be divided tidily into countless little plots. Perugia is a convenient transit hub for the rest of Umbria, and notable sites surround it like the spokes of a wagon wheel.

PERUGIA

Perugia ㉑ the capital city of this primarily rural region, is a stylish, dynamic place where chocolates and pasta are made and a modern urban atmosphere predominates. Its medieval centre, however, is worth a visit, and its art museum is among the best in the country. Perugia is 155km (94 miles) southwest of Florence via the A1 *autostrada* and RA6.

The main street, the Corso Vannucci, bisects the city and is a superb place to watch the Perugians go about their business. On this street is the **Palazzo dei Priori**, an enormous town hall. Built between the 13th and 14th centuries from local travertine stone, the Palazzo presents an imposing facade, with its Gothic doorway

⊙ PERUGINO

Perugino (1445–1523) is perhaps the greatest of the Umbrian painters. You'll see the best of his work in the city of Perugia, for which he was named. This Umbrian master also spent time working in Florence and Rome, key cities of the Italian Renaissance. His trademark limpid skies and ethereal landscapes, expressive of spirituality, can also be found in the paintings of his pupil, Raphael. To see Perugino paintings, you will want to stop at the Galleria Nazionale and the Collegio di Cambio (both in the Palazzo di Priori) in Perugia and the Accademia, the Galleria Palatina and the Uffizi in Florence.

and many rows of windows. On the upper floors is the **Galleria Nazionale** (daily 8.30am–7.30pm, closed Mon Nov–Mar; www.gallerianazionaleumbria.it), which contains a superb collection of Umbrian art. The 30-odd rooms offer a fascinating chronology of the origins and development of the region's art. A few works are especially noteworthy. Duccio's *Madonna and Child* has a quiet beauty. The triptych

Gubbio's Palazzo dei Consoli

Madonna and Child with Angels and Saints, by Fra Angelico, is boldly coloured in blue. Piero della Francesca's polyptych of *Saint Anthony* has a remarkably delicate Annunciation scene at the top of the main painting. And a group of altarpieces by Perugino shows the development of his style; note especially his *Pietà*, painted around 1475. At ground level of the Palazzo is the **Collegio del Cambio**, a well-preserved Renaissance guildhall with frescoes by Perugino at the height of his glory.

The Palazzo fronts on the **Piazza IV Novembre**. The Romans built a reservoir here; later, medieval citizens filled it in to create an open space that became the hub of the city. A lovely centrepiece is the 13th-century Fontana Maggiore. Designed by Fra Bevignate and built by Nicola and Giovanni Pisano, it collected water from an aqueduct for the townspeople's use. Sculpture depicting the city's history surrounds its base; note the lion and the griffin, symbols of Perugia.

The **Duomo** (daily 8am–12.30pm, 4–7pm), also on the piazza, has a rather plain facade and a surprisingly characterless interior. Although, displayed with great fanfare in the Cappella del Sant'Agnello, is one of the Duomo's most valued treasures – a ring that is allegedly the Virgin's wedding band.

GUBBIO

Medieval **Gubbio** ㉒ 39km (24 miles) northeast of Perugia on the SR298, is a bit remote, but well worth a visit. It is so well preserved that it has earned the nickname 'the Umbrian Siena'. But its location is what sets it apart: the Apennines tower behind it, a wild gorge courses through it and a bare plain stretches in front. The central square, the **Piazza Quaranta Martiri**, is named in honour of the victims of a Nazi reprisal for partisan activities. On the piazza, the Gothic church of **San Francesco** contains a fine series of frescoes depicting the life of the Virgin Mary. St Francis is supposed to have slept in the sacristy chapel during a visit here.

East of here along the Via della Repubblica is the **Palazzo dei Consoli** (daily, Apr–Oct 10am–1pm, 3–6pm, Nov–Mar 10am–1pm, 2.30–5.30pm; www.palazzodeiconsoli.it), a stone palace with battlements and a towering campanile that stands

Inspiring and spiritual Assisi

on the **Piazza Grande** and provides a wide view of the town and plain below. An archaeological museum inside contains a good collection of Roman artefacts, and the Eugubian Tablets, bronze tablets inscribed in the ancient Umbrian language.

But it would be a shame to spend too much time indoors in Gubbio. From the palace, you might wish to wander further east, to the **Duomo** (daily 7.15am–6pm) – step inside to admire its unusual interior vaulting, and then on to the adjacent **Palazzo Ducale** (Tue–Sun 8.30am–7.30pm), whose restored rooms have a calm Renaissance air. A street behind the palace leads up to **Monte Ingino**, which is topped by the Basilica di Sant Ubaldo and provides a fabulous view after a steep climb.

ASSISI

The birthplace of St Francis, (27km/17 miles east of Perugia on the SS75), **Assisi** ㉓ is one of the holiest and most popular pilgrimage sites in Italy. Don't be put off by its popularity: this tiered village, on the flanks of Monte Subasio above valleys of olive groves, has a visual and spiritual elegance that has survived the onslaught of postcard stands.

St Francis was born in the 12th century and was later given permission by the Pope to create a new monastic order. Shortly after his death in 1226 work began on the **Basilica di San Francesco** (donation; www.sanfrancescoassisi.org), a monumental building on the eastern edge of Assisi, containing some of the masterworks of Italian art. The following are a few highlights:

In the **lower church** (daily 6am–6.30pm) are Simone Martini's frescoes in the Cappella di San Martino; painted in the early 14th century, those in the outer chapel depict several saints, while those in the inner chapel trace the life of St Martin of Tours. They display the artist's skill at recreating richly patterned fabrics. Stairs halfway along the nave lead down to the

The beguiling medieval city of Todi

crypt where St Francis's plain coffin rests. The Cappella della Maddalena, the last chapel on the right, is decorated with frescoes by Giotto depicting the life of Mary Magdalene. Finally, note Cimabue's well-known portrait of St Francis in the right transept.

The **upper church** (daily 8.30am–5.45pm) is bright and spacious. Pride of place is given to Giotto's frescoes illustrating the life of St Francis. The 28 panels were probably completed at the end of the 13th century. Giotto was a member of St Francis's lay registry, and his paintings reveal enormous sympathy for this humble man. Note also the dramatic *Crucifixion* by Cimabue in the transept. In 1997 several earthquakes shook the church, causing the collapse of part of the ceiling. Thanks to the hard work of many dedicated restorers and some computer wizardry, the majority of the damaged frescoes have been restored.

Outside the church again, head east towards the **Piazza del Comune**. This was most likely the site of the Roman forum, and six Corinthian columns from the 1st-century BC Roman Temple of Minerva still stand here, incorporated into a rather humdrum church.

There is much more to see in Assisi, but two more sights deserve special mention. The **Rocca Maggiore** (daily, Nov–Mar 10am–4.30pm, Apr–May & Sept–Oct 10am–6.30pm,

June–Aug 9am–8pm) is set high above the city at the end of a maze of medieval lanes, north of the Piazza del Comune. The castle was probably erected on old defensive walls built by Charlemagne; what stands here today dates from the 14th century. And 4km (2.5 miles) outside the city walls, through the Portao Cappuccine, is **Eremo delle Carceri**, the hermitage where St Francis meditated and prayed. An interesting walk through the woods leads to the ancient oak tree under which Saint Francis preached sermons to the birds. Today the hermitage is still inhabited by Franciscan monks.

TODI AND SPOLETO

Around 47km (29 miles) south of Perugia down the SS3bis (E45), the marvellous hill town of **Todi ㉔** is worth a stop. Todi's central **Piazza del Popolo** has been lauded as the most perfect medieval square in Italy. Spacious, flanked by the Duomo and three 13th-century palaces, it has a visual unity and appeal that makes it unique.

Across the valley, east of Todi, is **Spoleto ㉕**, another Umbrian gem, set on terraces on the flank of a hill. This prosperous little town has a fine Roman amphitheatre, some lovely churches and a renowned annual festival. The Festival dei Due Mondi, started by composer Giancarlo Menotti in 1958, runs for two weeks late June to early July (www.festivaldispoleto.com), and draws a myriad of internationally known dance, music and theatre groups, plus some avant-garde companies. The festivities have spilled over into preceding months, when classical music is featured, and succeeding months, when opera takes over. Tickets and accommodation should be booked well in advance.

Spoleto provides other pleasures as well. On the edge of the lower town, **San Salvatore** (daily 7am–dusk), dating from the 4th century, is one of the oldest churches in Italy, somewhat musty, but highly atmospheric, with its Corinthian columns, bare walls and stone floors. Also in the lower town are the remains of a Roman amphitheatre. The Romans built special gutters to accommodate the flow of blood from their festivities.

In the upper town, the 12th-century **Duomo** (daily, Nov–Mar 8.30am–12.30pm, 3.30–6pm, Apr–Oct until 7pm), on the Piazza del Duomo, has an unusual mosaic facade, built in the early 13th century by Solsternus. Inside is a fresco cycle on the life of the Virgin by Filippo Lippi. This was his last work; he died in 1469, just before finishing it. Note especially the beautifully coloured *Coronation of the Virgin*, and the central panel, the *Dormition of Mary*, in which Filippo has painted himself wearing a black tunic and a white robe. Just east of the Duomo, take the Via del Ponte around the fortress to the **Ponte delle Torri**. This 13th-century engineering marvel stretches 230m (760ft) across a valley, supported by nine stone pillars.

ORVIETO

A nice way to approach **Orvieto** ㉖ some 86km (54 miles) southwest of Perugia, is via a very pretty road, the SS448, which cuts west from Todi and winds around Lago di Corbara. The A1 *autostrada* between Florence and Rome also zooms past the base of the city; Orvieto is 230km (130 miles) south of Florence.

While much of the volcanic rock in southern Umbria has been eroded by the Tiber and Paglia rivers, one spire remains unlevelled, and it is on this that Orvieto sits, towering over the valley floor more than 305m (1,000ft) below.

The city's **Duomo** (daily, Nov–Feb 7.30am–1pm, 2.30–5pm, Mar and Oct until 6pm, Apr–Sept until 7pm), set on the city's highest point, is its most spectacular sight, perhaps the most spectacular in all of Umbria. Its cornerstone was laid in the 13th century to mark the Miracle of Bolsena, in which a Bavarian priest on a pilgrimage to Rome witnessed transubstantiation – he saw blood dripping from the host onto a cloth as he attended mass in a church on nearby Lago di Bolsena. The cloth was taken to Pope Urban IV, who was in Orvieto at the time, and he ordered the construction of a great church to commemorate the event.

The dazzling facade of Orvieto's Duomo

The original architect was probably Arnolfo di Cambio, although work continued on the Duomo for some 300 years, and what stands today is an amalgam of some of the greatest talents of the period, including most notably Lorenzo Maitani. The facade consists of four huge pillars supporting a wild array of sculptures, spires and doorways. The pillars, designed by Maitani, depict detailed scenes from the Bible; note especially Cain killing Abel. Inside, head for the altar. To the right is the Cappella della Madonna di San Brizio, decorated with frescoes by Fra Angelico and Luca Signorelli. Fra Angelico completed two sections of the ceiling, showing Christ and the Prophets, in the 15th century and was then called away to Rome. Signorelli finished his work, then covered the walls with a remarkable series of frescoes. Note especially his *Last Judgement*, which provided inspiration for Michelangelo's painting in the Sistine Chapel, and his *Damned in Hell*, a terrifying scene depicting what may await the worst among us.

Tuscan produce for sale in San Gimignano

 # WHAT TO DO

Looking at some of the Western world's greatest artistic achievements – perhaps with time out for an excellent meal here and there – could well fill your days and nights in Tuscany and Umbria. There are, however, many other activities, from shopping to music festivals, with which to occupy your time. For some additional opportunities to combine travel with learning and pursuing special interests, see page 126.

SHOPPING

Whether it's high fashion, stationery, leather goods, ceramics, or one of the other products for which Italy is justifiably famous, you will find a wide selection throughout the regions.

FLORENTINE FAVOURITES

High fashion. Florence is next to Milan for its fashion sense. Many fashion shows are held here in the winter, and many designers have boutiques in the city, concentrated on and around Via Tornabuoni and Via della Vigna Nuova. Yes, these shops are expensive, but most Italian designer goods – whether an Armani suit or a Gucci bag – are less expensive in Florence than they would be in London or New York.

Fabrics. Tuscany has produced quality woollens, linens and other fabrics for hundreds of years. Prato, just north of Florence, is home to many important producers. An important historic fabrics store in Florence is the Casa dei Tessuti (www.casadeitessuti.com) on Via de' Pecori, a block away from the Duomo.

Gold and silver. Florentines are well known as silversmiths and goldsmiths, and they continue to dispense lovely jewellery from the expensive shops along the Ponte Vecchio. The Palazzo Pitti neighbourhood is a good spot to find silversmiths selling figurines, silverware and the like. You will also find many excellent jewellery shops on and around Via Tornabuoni, but what you won't find, except perhaps at a flea market, is bargain prices.

Leather goods. A leather centre since the Middle Ages, Florence continues to delight visitors with its vast array of jackets, as well as gloves, bags, shoes and other accessories. You may be tempted by the array and the prices at the Mercato San Lorenzo and the Mercato Nuovo, but you'll probably be less pleased with the quality. These markets are, however, good places to stock up on inexpensive and popular gifts, like lipstick cases and coin purses. An interesting place to shop for leather goods is the leather-working school attached to the church of Santa Croce (www.scuoladelcuoio.com). Some of the best shops are clustered along the Arno between the Ponte Vecchio and Via Tornabuoni.

Stationery. Paper goods are among the more interesting Florentine specialities. Journals, diaries, notebooks, decorative papers and the like are beautiful and well made. Some Florentine shops, such as Il Papiro (www.ilpapirofirenze.it) on Via dei Tavolini and Pineider (www.pineider.com) on Piazza de'Rucellai, sell their products across the globe, but their offerings tend to be less expensive here.

OTHER REGIONAL CRAFTS

You will find enticing goods in most towns throughout these two regions. The following places are especially well known for the products of their artisans.

You will have no difficulty finding the famous brightly coloured and patterned **Derutaware** ceramics for which the Umbrian town of Deruta is well known. There are numerous shops in the Old Town and on the roads leading into it. You can see the

Crafts for sale, Bagno di Vignoni

ceramics being made in the Fabbrica Maioliche Tradizionali (www.maiolichepeccetti.com) workshop at Via Tiberina Nord 37.

Artisans from Gubbio perfected the art of glazing **majolica** centuries ago, and today the town remains one of Italy's major ceramics centres. You can find excellent goods made by local artisans at various shops throughout town, including Fabbrica Mastro Giorgio, on Via Tifernate.

Dozens of shops around Volterra sell attractive **alabaster** objects. To see a nice representation of the output of the town's alabaster artisans, visit the Cooperativa Artieri Alabastro (www.artierialabastro.it) on Piazza dei Priori.

ANTIQUES AND FLEA MARKETS

Florence is one of Italy's major antiques centres, with many shops clustered across the Arno from the centre of the city, around Via Maggio. For high-quality antiques or attic cast-offs, you may also want to browse in the antiques fairs and flea markets in the following towns.

Arezzo. Antiques fair, one of Italy's largest, first weekend of every month in Piazza Grande.

Florence. Flea market every day in Piazza dei Ciompi. Artisan/flea market on Piazza Santo Spirito the second Sunday of the month (not in July and August). Huge fresh food/flea market

⊙ OUTLET SHOPPING

For serious bargain-hunters, Tuscany has two main outlet malls in the vicinity of Florence. Although they require a car or bus trip out of the city, dedicated shoppers can find significant discounts on their favourite Italian brands.

The Mall, Via Europa 8, Leccio Regello (daily 10am–7pm; www.themall.it). High-end stores include Armani, Bottega Veneta, Ermenegildo Zegna, Ferragamo, Gucci, Valentino and Roberto Cavalli, among others. Shuttle buses can be booked to take the 30-minute drive from Florence; or, for thriftier shoppers, SITA offers a public bus service that leaves approximately every 30 minutes from Florence's bus depot near the railway station.

Barberino, Via Meucci SNC, Barberino del Mugello (daily 10am–8/9pm; www.mcarthurglen.com). Part of the world-wide McArthurGlen chain, Barberino offers a mixture of more than 100 high-end and mid-priced brands. You'll find Adidas, Bruno Magli, Calzedonia, Coccinelle, D&G, Furla, Fornarina, Guess, Missoni, Pinko, Prada, Puma, Stefanel and United Colors of Benetton, among many others. Like The Mall, Barberino can be reached in about 30 minutes, either by shuttle bus or by the SITA bus service, which leaves from the bus depot near the main station in Florence.

in the Cascine Park on Tuesday morning.

Gubbio. Antiques fair, the third Sunday of the month.

Lucca. Antiques and flea market, one of Italy's best-attended, third weekend each month in and around Piazza San Giusto.

Montepulciano. Artisan fair, the second weekend of the month in Piazza Grande.

Pistoia. Antiques fair along Via Cavour and Via Bozzi, the second weekend of the month (none in July and August).

Pickled delights

WEEKLY MARKETS

Many Tuscans and Umbrians rely on their towns' produce markets to stock up on everything from salami to shoelaces. Held at least weekly and sometimes more often in most towns of any size, markets afford travellers a chance to discover and sample local foods and observe local customs. Most are held in the morning.

Florence (Mercato Centrale and Piazza Sant'Ambrogio), Pisa (Piazza delle Vettovaglie) and Perugia (Piazza Matteotti) all have markets that are open every day except Sunday. Some of the larger markets in the region that are held weekly include: Assisi, Saturday; Cortona, Saturday; Gubbio, Tuesday; Montepulciano, Thursday; Orvieto, Thursday and Saturday; Pienza, Friday; Portoferraio (Elba), Friday; Prato, Monday; San Gimignano, Thursday and Saturday; Siena, Wednesday; Volterra, Saturday.

SPORTS AND OUTDOOR ACTIVITIES

With their long summers and pleasant autumns and springs, Tuscans and Umbrians have ample opportunity to spend time outdoors. Here are some pursuits in which you might want to join them.

Swimming. The most enjoyable swimming is from the beaches on Elba, especially from the unspoiled strands around the hamlets of Nisporto and Nisportino. The best of the beaches on the mainland are probably those around San Vincenzo, south of Livorno. There are several beaches on the shores of Lago di Trasimeno in Umbria, though they tend to be reedy; the best one is at Castiglione del Lago on the western shore.

Golf. There are plenty of golf courses in Tuscany and Umbria.

Hiking trail to Eremo di Montesiepi

One of the best in the region is Golf dell'Ugolino close to Impruneta in Chianti country, tel: (055) 230 1009, www.golfu-golino.it; another is the Cosmopolitan Golf and Country Club, not far from Livorno, tel: (050) 33 633; www.cosmopolitangolf.it.

Hiking. In Tuscany, the mountainous regions of the northwest – the Garfagnana to the north of Lucca and the Apuan Alps around Carrara to the northwest – provide some of the most challenging hikes, with the town of Castelnuovo di Garfagnana making a good base. In the northeast, the rugged Apennine land of the Mugello is popular among hikers who follow the 'Springs of Florence Trekking' (SOFT) network, which consists of a huge central ring of trails and 22 secondary rings around the area. The tourist office in Borgo San Lorenzo (www.mugellotoscana. it/en) provides information on the different themed hikes, which can make for a few hours' or days' walking. In Umbria, the countryside around Spoleto is also good for hiking. Most tourist boards will provide a list of hikes in their area.

Horse-riding. The terrain along the Tuscan coast is quite popular with equestrians. Two stables are Rifugio Prategiano, in the town of Montieri near the city of Grosseto, tel: (0566) 997 700 and about a half hour journey south of Florence at Val d'Este, Il Paretaio, tel: (055) 805 9218, www.Ilparetaio.it. A list of equestrian centres in the Province of Florence can be downloaded from www.firenzeturismo.lt.

Spectator sports. Florence has a *calcio* (football) team that plays its home games at Stadio Artemio Franchi; tickets can be hard to come by but are available at the Club's box office or online at www.ticketone.it. If you are in Florence on or around the feast of St John (late June), you may want to catch the Calcio in Costume, where you can see a rough-and-tumble medieval version of the game played in period costume.

ENTERTAINMENT

MUSIC AND THE PERFORMING ARTS

Tuscany and Umbria host a number of events showcasing music and the performing arts. Check with local tourist boards (see page 133) for lists of events; in many towns you

Wine bars stay open late into the evening

may fortuitously stumble upon a one-evening-only concert or performance.

Florence has an autumn-to-spring schedule of concerts, operas and dance performances at its two major venues for the performing arts: the Teatro del Maggio, on Piazzale Vittorio Gui, and Teatro Verdi, on Via Ghibellina.

Tuscany and Umbria are favoured settings for many inter-nationally renowned music festivals. **Arezzo** hosts a multi-day summer music festival featuring contemporary Italian and international artists. **Città di Castello** draws visitors from around the world for its Festival delle Nazioni di Musica da Camera (International Chamber Music Festival) during the last week of August/beginning of September. **Fiesole** holds summer concerts in the Roman amphitheatre. **Florence** now spreads its Maggio Musicale (Musical May) into June as well, hosting concerts and dance performances in palazzos, churches and other atmospheric venues around the city. **Lucca** stages a rock and jazz festival throughout July, which takes place in Piazza Napoleone. Nearby **Torre del Lago** was Puccini's home and now hosts an opera festival in July and August dedicated to the famous composer.

Montepulciano hosts the Cantiere Internazionale d'Arte, a major music and theatre festival, in July. **Perugia** hosts two major musical festivals, Umbria Jazz in July and the Sagra Musicale Umbria in September. **Pistoia**'s Blues Festival, usually held in July, has become an important stop for international blues, jazz and rock artists. **Spoleto**'s Festival dei Due Mondi (Festival of Two Worlds) is one of the world's most highly acclaimed musical events, drawing classical artists, dancers and others at the end of June/beginning of July.

NIGHTLIFE

Italians pursue a 'piazza' culture, spending much of their social lives out and about, rather than in the comfort of their homes. Although there is not the raging pub and club scene that can be found in other countries, the larger cities offer a lively variety of pubs, bars and nightclubs. You'll also find plenty of cosy wine bars that offer a large wine and cheese selection and stay open late into the evening.

Appreciative of their agreeable weather, local people are also apt to go out for a stroll (passeggiata) either before or after dinner, often stopping off for a gelato.

CHILDREN'S TUSCANY AND UMBRIA

At first sight, Tuscany and Umbria do not appear an immediate choice for kids, but there are some child-friendly activities on offer. There are many good parks and nature reserves and

Fountains are fun

numerous opportunities for horse-riding, cycling and swimming. Much of the coast is also great for children. The resorts of Viareggio and Elba are well set up, and most coastal cities have permanent funfairs. Finding a place to eat with the kids in tow is never a problem in Italy. The area is full of ice-cream parlours and child-friendly restaurants.

In **Florence**, the Egyptian collection at the Archaeological Museum (www.florence-museum.com) near the Accademia is full of mummies, and the Museo Galileo (www.museogalileo.it) near the Uffizi has working models of Galileo's experiments. The Palazzo Vecchio offers child-friendly palace tours and fun workshops, such as fresco painting. The Boboli Gardens and the Cascine are the two main parks, where kids can let off steam, whilst one of the few children's playgrounds is found in Piazza dell'Azeglio.

At the **Parco di Pinocchio** at Collodi near Pisa (www.pinocchio.it) children can relive the adventures of the famous puppet. There is a small but interesting **zoo** in Pistoia (www.zoodipistoia.it). Many towns in Tuscany and Umbria have medieval towers to climb; at **Lucca** kids can ride a bike around the medieval walls, and there are funicular railways at **Gubbio** and **Orvieto**. Near Livorno, **Cavallino Matto** (www.cavallinomatto.it) is the largest theme park in the region, chock full with rides, games and shows.

CALENDAR OF EVENTS

February Several towns celebrate *carnevale*, notably San Gimignano, with a colourful procession, and Viareggio, where celebrations last three weeks.

Holy Week Solemn celebrations in Assisi and in Gubbio, with a procession of the Dead Christ, accompanied by chanting, on Good Friday.

Easter Scoppio del Carro (Explosion of the Cart) in Florence: after high mass in the Duomo a mechanical dove is released from the altar and sets off fireworks in the piazza outside.

First weekend after 1 May Calendimaggio in Assisi: a three-day festival with colourful traditional parades and a singing contest.

Mid-May Festa dei Ceri: in Gubbio's Corso dei Ceri, a procession of torch-bearers races to the top of Mount Ingino.

June Giostra dell'Archidado: re-enactments of a 14th-century crossbow tournament and a Renaissance-style wedding in Cortona.

Third Saturday in June Giostra del Saracino: old-fashioned medieval jousting in Arezzo (also in September).

Ascension Day Festa del Grillo *(cricket)* in Cascine Park, Florence.

16–17 June Pisa celebrates San Ranieri by lining the Arno with candles.

24 June Florence honours San Giovanni with fireworks; historically costumed football teams play in Piazza Santa Croce's Calcio Storico.

2 July In Siena, jockeys from the city's *contrade* (neighbourhoods) race around the Campo, the central piazza (it is run again on 16 August).

25 July Pistoia revives its Giostra del Orso, once a bear-baiting contest; today the event features horsemen who attack bear-shaped targets.

15 August (Ferragosto) Cortona celebrates the Assumption with a feast in which tons of Valdichiana beef are served in the public gardens.

Mid-September Luminari di Santa Croce in Lucca: the Volto Santo (a figure of Christ) is taken through the streets in a candlelit procession.

3 and 4 October Assisi celebrates the feast of St Francis with processions, outdoor meals and musical performances.

Late October–November Gubbio stages a lively truffle fair.

26 December Prato celebrates Santo Stefano with a showing of its famous relic, the girdle of the Virgin, with much pomp and ceremony.

EATING OUT

The cuisines of Tuscany and Umbria are highly revered throughout food-focused Italy. In general, the cuisine is rustic and simple, relying heavily upon fresh vegetables, legumes (pulses), meat and game. The only elaborate sauces you are likely to encounter will be on pasta – meats are usually just seasoned and served grilled or roasted. Olive oil and wine also play key roles in the Mediterranean diet.

WHERE TO EAT

Italy has three traditional types of place to eat: a *trattoria*, a *ristorante* or an *osteria*. At first they may appear to be similar, and this is increasingly true, but to Italians they signify different types of dining experiences. A *trattoria* is more casual, serving basic regional dishes in an informal setting. *Trattorie* are often family-owned and have no frills. A *ristorante* implies somewhat fancier décor, more formal service, and more elaborate and expensive food. To make things more confusing, the *osteria* is historically a tavern-like wine shop where you can buy a glass of wine and perhaps a hunk of cheese, but the word is now used almost interchangeably with *ristorante* or *trattoria*.

Yet another type of eating establishment is the *tavola calda* or *rosticceria*, both of which are cafeteria-style places where several selections of hot dishes are prepared daily and served from a counter. You generally pay in advance and show the receipt to someone working behind the counter, who prepares a plate for you.

Although pizza has become a national dish, it is not one for which these regions are particularly famous. Eating in a *pizzeria* costs considerably less than in a *ristorante* or *trattoria*, and they generally serve only pizza and appetisers.

In general, a *ristorante* or *trattoria* serves both lunch and dinner. Lunch is generally from 12.30 to 3pm, and dinner from 7.30 to 11pm. Most establishments close one day a week and occasionally for lunch or dinner immediately preceding or following that day. Most Italian eating establishments have the good sense to close for holidays *(ferie)* once or even twice a year. Some restaurants close for at least two weeks around 15 August and sometimes another week or two in the winter.

Caffès are a good place for a light snack

WHAT TO EAT

You will notice that just about all menus are divided into more or less the same categories (to an Italian, these are the essential elements of a decent meal): *antipasti* (appetisers), *primi* (first courses), *secondi* (second courses), *contorni* (side dishes) and *dolci* (desserts).

Italians take eating seriously. The whole dining experience is to be enjoyed, and restaurateurs expect their non-Italian patrons to approach it in the same way, so never try getting away with ordering only an *antipasto*. Ordering just a pasta dish or a *secondo* and *contorno* is acceptable, especially at lunch.

Antipasto means 'before the meal', and these selections are usually served in small portions. Many restaurants offer an *antipasto misto* (mixed appetiser) that is often served buffet-style from a table laden with such dishes as *melone con prosciutto* (ham and melon) or grilled vegetables, and *insalata caprese* (mozzarella, tomatoes and fresh basil).

Typical Tuscan *antipasti*: *crostini*, tomatoes or liver pâté on toasted bread; *prosciutto di cinghiale*, ham from wild boar; *finocchiona*, pork sausage laced with fennel.

Typical Umbrian *antipasti*: *bruschetta*, toasted bread topped with garlic and olive oil, sometimes with chopped tomatoes as well; *prosciutto di Norcia*, ham from the town of Norcia, Umbria's foremost producer of pork; *schiacciata*, a flat bread sometimes topped with onions and other vegetables.

Il primo is the first course, and in Tuscany and Umbria that generally means hearty soup or pasta (increasingly you will also find risotto).

Typical Tuscan *primi*: *acquacotta*, onion soup that is a speciality of Arezzo; *minestrone alla fiorentina*, a vegetable soup with beans; *panzanella*, a bread salad often found on summer menus, whose ingredients also include tomatoes and basil; *pappardelle con lepre* or *con cinghiale*, broad noodles topped with a rich sauce made from hare or wild boar; *ribollita*, a rich vegetable soup with bread mixed into it, usually served in winter and often made from leftover vegetables, hence the name, which means 'reboiled'; *cacciuco*, a rich fish soup that is reason in itself to travel to Livorno.

Food festivals

Sagras are food festivals held throughout the year, usually in small country towns. Local people join together to cook dishes that feature a star ingredient (artichokes, chestnuts, wild boar, truffles, etc) in a casual and lively setting. Lists of events are available at www.festivalsinitaly.com.

Italian staples: bread and wine

Typical Umbrian *primi*: *minestra di farro*, a vegetable soup; *tagliatelle con funghi porcini*, thick noodles with wild mushrooms; *pici*, a fat, short spaghetti usually served with tomato sauce; *baggiana*, a soup of fava beans and tomatoes.

Il secondo is the main dish of meat or fish, usually meat in Tuscany and Umbria, and often beefsteak, pork, rabbit or game birds in both regions. Some typical dishes of both regions are *porchetta*, roast suckling pig, often sold from stalls at markets or on roadsides; *cinghiale*, wild boar, usually roasted or made into sausages called *salciccia*; *fritto misto*, a mixed grill including lamb chops and sweetbreads, among other meats; *anatra*, duck; and *girarrosto*, a spit of roast game birds.

Typical Tuscan *secondi*: *trippa alla fiorentina*, tripe with tomato sauce; *baccala alla livornese*, salt cod, a speciality of Livorno; and *bistecca alla fiorentina*, a T-bone steak grilled rare, Florence's claim to culinary fame.

Ice cream, always a favourite

Typical Umbrian *secondi*: *frittata di tartufi*, an omelette made with truffles; *regina in porchetta*, carp from Lago di Trasimeno, covered with herbs and baked in an oven.

Il contorno is the vegetable course. It's always ordered separately, as vegetables and salad are never included with a *secondo*. Usually only a few items are offered, but they tend to be fresh from the market. *Fagioli*, beans – especially white beans – are a favourite. Salads (*insalate*) are straightforward and tend to come in two varieties: *insalata verde*, a simple green salad, or *insalata mista*, green leaves with mixed vegetables.

Il dolce is dessert, a course that is not among Italy's greatest culinary achievements, but ice cream (*gelato*) is reliably delicious when it is home-made, and *biscotti* are sweet biscuits, often almond flavoured, that are dipped in *vinsanto*, a sweet wine. Most restaurants offer *tiramisù*, a dessert made with sponge biscuits dipped in coffee and mascarpone cream. Many towns have their own sweet specialities that show up on menus and in shops.

Typical Tuscan *dolci*: *cantucci*, small versions of *biscotti*, a delicious speciality of Prato; *panforte*, a Sienese cake made with nuts and candied fruit.

Typical Umbrian *dolci*: *gelato ai Baci,* creamy ice cream with Perugia's famous Perugina chocolates folded into it; *roccoiata*, a cake with a rich filling of walnuts, almonds, raisins and honey, is a speciality of Assisi.

BARS, CAFFÈS AND GELATERIE

In Italy, bars are not solely dedicated to alcoholic beverages. They usually serve wine and spirits as well as soft drinks, mineral water and, especially, enormous quantities of coffee. Incidentally, Italians consider a *cappuccino* to be a morning drink and would not dream of ordering one after dinner, but *espresso* can be drunk at any time of day. Drinks are accompanied in the morning by croissant-like pastries (*cornetti* or *brioche*, often filled with jam, custard or chocolate) and throughout the day by little snacks or sandwiches (*panini*).

You do not usually pay the people serving behind the counter. Instead, you decide what you want, go to the cash desk (*la cassa*) and pay in advance; the cashier will give you a receipt that you present to the bar staff when you order. Bars keep long hours, usually opening around 7.30 or 8am to serve breakfast, and remaining open until around 8 or 8.30pm, after serving the pre-dinner aperitif.

A *caffè* is usually an elegant or trendy establishment that Americans or the British might call a tearoom. Many towns have at least one august *caffè*; there are two in Florence on the Piazza della Repubblica: Caffè Gilli and Caffè Paszkowski. A *caffè* usually

Gelaterie

Most towns are blessed with at least one *gelateria*, a shop that sells only ice cream and *sorbetto*, which is a refreshing and less fattening alternative, made with ice often mixed with fresh fruit. A *gelateria* worth seeking out in Florence is the world-famous Vivoli on Via Isole di Stinche near Santa Croce.

Italy is a nation of coffee drinkers

serves pastries and *gelato* and sometimes light meals, accompanied by coffee, tea or a glass of wine.

BEVERAGES

Italian beer is extremely palatable; ask for a *birra nazionale* and you will probably be served a bottle of Peroni. Many imported brands are also available. Draught beer *(birra alla spina)* is often imported and quite a bit more expensive.

Tap water is generally drinkable throughout Tuscany and Umbria, and in many rural settings comes fresh from wells. Even so, most Italians prefer to drink mineral water *(acqua minerale)*. In restaurants you will be offered *acqua frizzante, con gas* or *gassata*, all of which mean mineral water 'with gas', which English speakers know better as 'sparkling water'; or *acqua naturale* or *non gassata*, still mineral water.

Refreshing alternatives include *spremuta*, freshly squeezed orange or lemon juice, to which you can add sugar and water to taste. *Granite* are wonderful concoctions of crushed ice to which fresh fruit juice or other flavourings are added; a *caffè granita* is a glass of coffee-permeated ice topped with whipped cream. This summery treat is available in most *gelaterie* and some bars. Among hot drinks, coffee is by far the most popular choice, but tea *(tè)* is widely available, served with milk *(con latte)* or lemon *(con limone)* or even cold *(freddo)* in summer.

WINE

Wine has, for hundreds of years, played an important role in Tuscan life. The world-famous Chianti wine denomination dates back to 1716 when Grand Duke Cosimo de' Medici III himself designated the specific area that was allowed to call its wine Chianti. The wine gained popularity when Baron Ricasoli, a wealthy landowner and part-time politician, began to experiment with its composition and entered his new Sangiovese, Canaiolo and Malvasia grape combination in the Paris wine exhibition of 1878.

These days, the area, which has had its geographical boundaries carefully specified, is completely covered with vineyards. Wine producers must follow a series of regulations before their wine can gain the Chianti denomination and bear the black cockerel logo.

⊘ RATING THE WINES

Italian wines are classified with four ratings. DOCG (Denominazione di Origine Controllata Garantita) indicates that a wine is from an established wine-producing region and maintains very high standards of quality. DOC (Denominazione di Origine Controllata) ensures that a wine is from an established area and meets the standards of that area; it is guaranteed to be a quality wine, but of a lesser quality than a DOCG one. IGT (Indicazione Geografica Tipica) was created in the 1990s in response to the modern practice of producing quality wines that deviate from the traditional production rules. *Vino da tavola* (VDT), the fourth classification, more or less denotes a good table wine from a reputable producer.

Tuscan wines enjoy a worldwide reputation

Chianti may be Tuscany's most famous wine, but Brunello, from vineyards around Montalcino, is widely considered its best. Deep, ruby red and robust, it must be played off against the strong taste of steak or game. The region's third contender is Montepulciano, a lovely, fruity, easy-on-the-palate red from the town of the same name.

Tuscany's best white wine is Vernaccia di San Gimignano. Recently, Tuscan producers have been experimenting with foreign grapes like merlot and cabernet sauvignon, and produced some delicious wines. If you can afford to splash out, try the Sassicaia, Cepparello or Ornellaia.

Though less famous than Tuscan wines, the Umbrian varieties can hold their own. The best are the delicate whites from Orvieto, notably the dry Orvieto Classico. Those from Montefalco, especially Sagrantino di Montefalco, are the region's best reds.

TO HELP YOU ORDER...

Vorrei una tavola per due/tre/quattro persone. I would like a table for two/three/four people.

Avete un menu? Do you have a menu?

Quanto costa? How much is it?

Il conto, per favore. The bill, please.

...AND READ THE MENU

aglio garlic
agnello lamb
basilico basil
birra beer
bistecca steak
bollito misto an array of boiled meats
bresaolo dried salt beef
brodo clear broth
burro butter
caffè coffee
calamari squid
Carciofi artichokes
cervo venison
cinghiale wild boar
cipolle onions
coniglio rabbit
cozze mussels
fagioli beans
fegato liver
finocchio fennel
formaggio cheese
frittata omelette
frutti di mare seafood
funghi mushrooms
gamberetti prawns
gelato ice cream
insalata salad
lepre hare
lumache snails
maiale pork

manzo beef
melanzane aubergine
minestra soup
olio oil
ossobuco shin of veal
pancetta bacon
pane bread
panna cream
patate potatoes
peperoni peppers
pesce fish
piccione pigeon
piselli peas
polipo octopus
pollo chicken
polpette meatballs
pomodori tomatoes
prosciutto ham
riso rice
rognoni kidneys
saltimbocca veal escalope with ham
spiedino skewers of meat
spinaci spinach
tè tea
uova eggs
verdura green vegetables
vitello veal
vino wine
vongole clams
zuppa di pesce fish soup

PLACES TO EAT

Unless indicated otherwise, these restaurants are open for lunch and dinner. We have used the following symbols to give an indication of the price of a three-course meal, excluding wine, per person. For additional restaurants in Florence, see the *Berlitz Pocket Guide to Florence*.

€€€€	over 60 euros
€€€	40–60 euros
€€	25–40 euros
€	below 25 euros

FLORENCE

Acqua al 2 €€ *Via della Vigna Vecchia 40r, tel: (055) 284 170,* www.acquaal 2.it. Closed Mon lunch. Located just behind the Bargello, this is a wonderful place to sample Florentine specialities, since many of the meals are served as *assaggi*, or sampling plates. The *assaggio di primi* is a meal in itself, with five different kinds of pasta that change daily. It's popular with locals and tourists.

Belle Donne €€ *Via delle Belle Donne 16r, tel: (055) 238 2609,* www.belle donneosteria.it. This tiny place can be difficult to find as there is no sign outside the door, but look for rustic Tuscan tradition combined with elegance and intimacy. You may end up sharing a table with fellow diners but the food is good, which is chosen from a list of tempting Tuscan specials, and that's what counts here.

Il Cibreo €€€€ *Via del Verrocchio 8r, tel: (055) 234 1100,* www.cibreo.com. Closed Mon. Justly famed restaurant not far from Santa Croce. 'Modern' Tuscan cooking with no pasta, but a superb selection of appetisers, soups and polenta dishes. The chocolate cake is legendary. Just around the corner at Via de' Macchi 112r, Cibreo Trattoria is a good cheaper option.

Enoteca Pinchiorri €€€€ *Via Ghibellina 87, tel: (055) 242 777,* www. enotecapinchiorri.it. Closed Sun–Mon, dinner only. Elegant, formal and expensive, this restaurant, just a short walk north from Santa Croce, receives some of Italy's highest marks for its nouvelle Tuscan cuisine as well as for the surroundings – a sumptuous Renaissance palace with frescoed ceilings.

Fishing Lab Alle Murate €€€€ *Via del Proconsolo 16r, tel: (055) 240 618,* www.fishinglab.it/en/firenze. Located close to the Duomo, as it says on the tin, this interesting restaurant is all about seafood cooked in creative ways. The dining space itself is also interesting, with original medieval frescos on the walls and vaulted ceilings that strangely complement the contemporary feel.

IO – Osteria Personale €€€ *Borgo San Frediano 167r, tel: (055) 933 1341,* www.io-osteriapersonale.it. Closed Sun, dinner only. Tradition meets chic among wood panelled ceilings, brick walls and sparsely elegant table settings at this Oltrarno spot – a nod to the sophisticated food to follow. Owner Matten Fantini chats happily with diners and draws whimsical art of the day's dishes onto chalkboards. A tasting menu is available.

Il Santo Bevitore €€ *Via di Santo Spirito 66r, tel: (055) 211 264,* www.il-santobevitore.com. Seemingly informal with wooden tables and simple candlelit setting, this restaurant, in the tiny streets of Oltrarno, takes great care in its choice of quality ingredients and presentation. Dishes are a modern interpretation of traditional Tuscan recipes.

Sostanza (aka Il Troia) €€ *Via del Porcellana 25r, tel: (055) 212 691.* Closed Sun. Florence's oldest restaurant, just off Borgo Ognissanti, is to be enjoyed as much for the experience of sharing a communal table with travellers from all over the world as for its excellent, straightforward food. The nickname is a giveaway for what to expect – *troia* means trough, and there is a lot of good-natured fun in watching so many happy diners digging into such hearty Tuscan favourites as *ribollita* (a hearty soup) and grilled chops.

Trattoria Katti €€ *Via Faenza 31, tel: (055) 295 274,* www.trattoriakatti-firenze.com. This jewel of a restaurant offers a wide selection of simple yet masterful Tuscan dishes, using the finest ingredients, and cooked to perfection. Owner Signora Maria, her daughter Katti and the chef Francesco are extremely warm and friendly people who work hard to ensure their guests enjoy their meal. The tiramisu is divine, made by Maria herself.

Trattoria Za-Za €€ *Piazza del Mercato Centrale 26r, tel: (055) 215 411,* www.trattoriazaza.it. The walls of this typical Florentine eatery, just across from the lively food market, are lined with Chianti bottles and photos of famous and not-so-famous patrons, both past and present. With market-fresh ingredients so near at hand, the food is delicious. *Trippa* (tripe) is one of the excellent and typically Florentine dishes on the menu.

REST OF TUSCANY

Arezzo

Buca di San Francesco €€ *Piazza San Francesco 1, tel: (0575) 23 271,* www.bucadisanfrancesco.it. Closed Tue, Mon dinner and part of July. *Buca* means 'cellar', and this atmospheric restaurant, an Arezzo institution, owes much of its fame to the frescoed rooms in the cellars of the centuries-old buildings it occupies. A good way to sample the offerings of the kitchen is with the *saporita di Bonconte*, a sort of mixed grill featuring a selection of nicely prepared meats: some grilled, some roasted, some fried.

La Lancia d'Oro €€€ *Piazza Grande 18, tel: (0575) 21 033,* www.ristorante lanciadoro.it. Closed Sun dinner and Mon in winter. Located under the Vasari Loggia facing onto a beautiful piazza, the cuisine is a mix of traditional Tuscan and modern dishes, like guinea fowl with caramelised grapes and liver on Genoese bread. Dessert is delightful here, too.

Cortona

La Grotta €€ *Piazza Baldelli 3, tel: (0575) 630 271,* www.trattorialagrotta. it. Closed Tue. In summer, try to arrive early in order to procure one of the five or six tables next to the fountain in the little alleyway, off Cortona's main square, that leads to this homely *trattoria*. The stone, brick and wood interior, on several levels, is also appealing. Wherever you sit, you may think you're in heaven when you try the mouthwatering home-made desserts, such as lemon cake.

Lucca

Ristorante Buca di Sant'Antonio €€€ *Via della Cervia 3, tel: (0583) 55 881,* www.bucadisantantonio.it. Closed Sun evening and Mon. What is probably Lucca's most famous restaurant has been serving food for more than 200 years and welcomes diners in a cosy maze of intimate rooms where musical instruments and books line the walls. A speciality of the house is roast kid *(capretto)*, often preceded by ravioli stuffed with courgette and ricotta cheese.

Trattoria da Leo €€ *Via Tegrimi 1, tel: (0583) 492 236,* www.trattoriadaleo. it. At this popular family-run trattoria you can eat in the dining room, with its pastel walls and wooden furnishings, or on the simple but shaded terrace. The owners pride themselves on making guests feel at home, sometimes pulling up a chair and chatting when the meal is over. The simple Tuscan dishes are greatly appreciated by those who want good home-cooking at a reasonable price.

Montepulciano

Le Logge del Vignola €€€ *Via delle Erbe 6, tel: (0578) 717 290,* www.le loggedelvignola.com. Closed Tue. A tiny restaurant with top level service and excellent food. The menu may seem rather short, but the dishes change according to the season, and always feature the freshest ingredients, locally sourced whenever possible. Top marks go to the dishes that incorporate Chianti's famous Chianina beef. There's also an extensive wine selection.

Pienza

Dal Falco € *Piazza Dante Alighieri 3, tel: (0578) 748 551,* www.ristorante dalfalco.it. Closed Fri. This relaxed *trattoria*, popular with residents of this lovely town, is in a modern building just steps away from the elegant Renaissance city centre. In warm weather you can eat on a pleasant terrace outside, and at other times in a dining room where the décor is contemporary but where decidedly old-style cuisine is served. A large selection of meat and game is grilled over an open fire.

Pisa

Da Bruno €€€ *Via Luigi Bianchi 12, tel: (050) 560 818,* www.anticatrattoria dabruno.it. Closed Wed lunch and Tue. Though beamed ceilings, tiled floors and a homely smattering of paintings on the walls lend this pleasant *trattoria* a rustic feel, it is actually an easy walk from the Duomo and the famous Leaning Tower. The Pisan menu includes *zuppa alla pisana*, a thick vegetable soup, and fresh fish.

Pistoia

Lo Storno € *Via del Lastrone 8, tel: (0573) 26 193.* Closed Sun dinner and Tue. This small, noisy and cheerful restaurant has the distinction of occupying premises that have been serving food and drink for more than 600 years. In the current manifestation, only a few pasta and main dishes are offered, all of them delicious and, with such choices as *ribollita*, rooted deep in Tuscan tradition.

Prato

La Veranda €€ *Via dell'Arco 10, tel: (0574) 38 235,* www.ristorantela veranda.il. Closed Sun and Mon. Looks are deceiving at this popular restaurant near the 13th-century Castello dell'Imperatore. The décor is a bit formal but service is friendly, and the atmosphere is casual and welcoming to families, who enjoy a large array of *antipasti* and traditional Tuscan specialities.

San Gimignano

Le Vecchie Mura €€ *Via Piandornella 15, tel: (0577) 940 270,* www.vec-chiemura.it. Closed Tue. A former stable building with stone walls and a vaulted ceiling provides a cosy setting for a meal, made all the more inviting by a contemporary look. The house speciality is *cinghiale*, the wild boar that roam the hills of Tuscany, which can be savoured in the form of grilled steaks, stewed in Vernaccia wine, or as an ingredient in rich pasta sauces. The terrace beside the restaurant offers panoramic views.

Siena

Osteria le Logge €€€ *Via del Porrione 33, tel: (0577) 48 013,* www.osteria lelogge.it. Closed Sun. One of Siena's most popular restaurants spills over two floors of a centuries-old house near the Campo and out onto a terrace for warm-weather dining. The service is efficient and friendly. An unusual *primo* is a house speciality, *malfatti* (spinach and cheese gnocchi). *Malfatti* doesn't mean 'badly made' but indicates that the gnocchi are unevenly shaped. The main courses stick to such substantial dishes as rabbit with blackberry sauce and guinea fowl cooked in red wine.

La Prosciutteria € *Via Magalotti 1, tel: (0577) 42 026.* Closed Sat. Split across a few rustic rooms with brick walls, La Prosciutteria has one of the finest selections of sandwiches, local cheeses, cured meats and antipasti in the city, perfect for sharing alongside a bottle of Italian red wine. A must-visit lunch spot for a truly authentic Tuscan experience.

Tre Cristi €€€ *Vicolo di Provenzano 1/7, tel: (0577) 280 608,* www.trecristi. com. Closed Sun. Though it's been a long time since this cosy *trattoria* served only the residents of the surrounding houses, the two long rooms adorned with paintings and wall plaques representing the town's *contrade*, and lined with wood benches, retain a friendly, neighbourhood feel. In warm weather, the place to eat is the terrace. Wherever you sit, you can pick from the wonderful assortment of *starters and* then move on to one of the signature fish dishes.

Volterra

Etruria €€ *Piazza dei Priori 6–8, tel: (0588) 86 064.* With a wonderful location on the lovely main piazza and named after Volterra's early inhabitants, the Etruria is reputed to be the best restaurant in town. It lives up to this reputation with an attractive frescoed interior and an excellent kitchen that sends out a large assortment of *crostini* to begin, followed by such hefty fare as *pappardelle di lepre* (pasta with rich hare sauce) and grilled steaks and chops. It also does a good fixed-price menu. Reservations are recommended.

UMBRIA

Assisi

La Stalla € *Via Eremo delle Carceri 24, tel: (075) 812 317.* Closed Wed. You will have to drive to this restaurant, or make the 1.5km (1-mile) trip on foot, but after all, the countryside location is what this restaurant, housed in what was once a livestock stable, is all about. The food, much of it prepared on an open fire, matches the countrified décor with its concentration on hearty portions of grilled meats and excellent sausages. Cash only.

Gubbio

Taverna del Lupo €€€ *Via Ansidei 21, tel: (075) 927 4368,* www.tavernadellupo.it. A Gubbian landmark, the Lupo is huge, seating around 200 in what still manages to remain a cosy environment, and so popular there is rarely an empty table. The Umbrian specialities include pasta with truffles.

Orvieto

Del Moro – Aronne €€ *Via San Leonardo 7, tel: (0763) 342 763,* www.trattoriadelmoro.info. Closed Tue. Set in three cosy rooms, this charming trattoria is one of Orvieto's most historic restaurants. The atmosphere is rustic, simple and welcoming and the home-cooked local food is always full of intense flavours. A speciality is the pappardelle and wild boar finished off with shaved truffles.

Le Grotte del Funaro €€ *Via Ripa Serancia 41, tel: (0763) 343 276,* www.grottedelfunaro.com. Closed Mon. It's difficult to know what deserves more praise here: the Umbrian cooking or the amazing location. Home-made pastas and grilled meats are often topped with the region's truffles, and you can enjoy them in a tufa cave *(grotte)* etched out in the mountain. If you are really hungry, try the *grigliata mista*, a mixed grill of lamb, wild boar, pork and sausages. Pizzas are also available.

Perugia

Il Falchetto €€ *Strada Fontana La Trinità 2/d, tel: (075) 573 1775*, www. ilfalchetto.it. Closed Mon. This peaceful eatery, just outside the centre, is set in the Umbrian green hills and serves excellent food at very fair prices. The home-made gnocchi, here called *falchetti*, are wonderful, and can be followed with a selection of grilled meats and vegetables.

La Taverna €€ *Via delle Streghe 8, tel: (075) 572 4128*, www.ristorante-lataverna.com. Next to the Teatro Pavone, this two-level restaurant has a refined and extremely romantic air, with candles flickering beneath the barrel-vaulted ceilings. Truffles *(tartufi)* appear atop some of the pasta dishes, as do less expensive but exquisite wild mushrooms *(funghi porcini)*.

Spoleto

Il Tartufo €€ *Piazza Garibaldi 24, tel: (0743) 40 236*, www.ristoranteiltartufo. it. Closed Mon and Sun dinner. *Tartufo* means truffle, and in Spoleto's oldest and most renowned restaurant (it has been run continuously by the same family since 1927), classical music will waft discreetly over your table as your enjoy the namesake fungi, prepared in one of many different ways. Sprinkled atop pasta dishes or slices of tender veal *(vitello)*, truffles add an exquisite flavour and make for a memorable dining experience.

Todi

Umbria €€€ *Via San Bonaventura 13, tel: (075) 894 2737*, www.ristorante umbria.it. Closed Tue. This restaurant has the best views in the region. Especially from the vine-shaded terrace, the views seem to extend for ever across the undulating Umbrian hills. The interior dining room, with its open hearth and wood-beamed ceilings, is warm and inviting, as is the cuisine. Wild boar is roasted over an open fire, and you can start with some hearty *primi* that include *polenta* laced with *funghi porcini* or with truffles.

A-Z TRAVEL TIPS

A SUMMARY OF PRACTICAL INFORMATION

A

ACCOMMODATION

One of the pleasures of travelling in Tuscany and Umbria is enjoying some of the excellent accommodation, which ranges from luxurious villas to modest country retreats to old-fashioned town-centre hotels. Another popular choice is the *agriturismo*, or farm stay. To be labelled as such, a property must have fewer than 30 beds and earn most of its income from agricultural pursuits. As a result, you are pretty much guaranteed a stay on a genuine farm, though rooms and prices can vary greatly (try www.agriturismo.net).

Tourist information offices (see page 133) can provide a detailed list of nearby hotels and *agriturismi*. The internet has made it much easier to locate the accommodation that best suits your needs, with scores of agencies and hotel or villa owners promoting their properties through websites with photographs, descriptions and comments from previous guests.

> I'd like a single/double room. **Vorrei una camera singola/matrimoniale or doppia**
> With bath/shower **Con bagno/doccia**
> What is the price per night? **Quanto costa per una notte?**

AIRPORTS

Tuscany is served by two international airports, one in Pisa (8km west of Florence) and one in Florence; the latter mostly handles flights from London and other European cities, while Pisa has flights from a wider variety of UK airports. Travellers to Umbria are best served by Rome's airports and the centrally located one in Perugia. Those travelling to northern or eastern Umbria could also consider the airports in Bologna and Ancona.

Pisa's Aeroporto Galileo Galilei (PSA) is connected to Pisa Centrale train station by the PisaMover (daily 6am–midnight; every 5–8 minutes;

€2.70) from where regular trains leave for Florence (journey time varies between 50 and 80 minutes depending on the train you take; €8.40). For airport information: tel: (050) 849 300, www.pisa-airport.com.

Amerigo Vespucci Airport (FLR) in **Florence** is 5km (3 miles) northwest of the city in Peretola. A bus connects the airport with the bus station in central Florence (journey time: 30 minutes; from 5am–11pm; €6). For airport information: tel: (055) 306 1830, www.aeroporto.firenze.it.

St Francis of Assisi Airport (PEG) in **Perugia** offers flights from a limited range of destinations, including Ryanair flights from London Stansted. The airport shuttle bus, which connects with the train station in the centre of Perugia, costs €8. For airport information: tel: (075) 592 141, www.airport.umbria.it.

Rome is served by two airports: Leonardo da Vinci (better-known as Fiumicino, the town where it is located 30km/18 miles southwest of Rome on the Mediterranean) and Ciampino, closer to the city and used mostly for charter and low-cost flights.

Leonardo da Vinci (FCO; www.adr.it) handles dozens of international flights a day. The airport is exceptionally well served by public transport. The Leonardo Express leaves from a station in the terminal complex for Rome's Termini train station (every 15 minutes between 6.30am and 11pm; €14).

From Ciampino (CIA; www.ciampinoairport.co.uk), you can take a coach (www.terravision.eu) from outside arrivals that leaves approximately once an hour for Rome's Stazione Termini (journey time: 40 minutes; €6 one way, cheaper if pre-booked). From Stazione Termini you can make connections to Florence, Perugia and other points throughout Tuscany and Umbria (see page 133).

If you plan to rent a car while visiting Italy, you will find it convenient to pick one up at Leonardo da Vinci's car-hire facilities and follow signs to the GRA, the motorway that encircles Rome, which in turn takes you to the A1 *autostrada*, the motorway that runs up and down the country, connecting Rome with such cities in Tuscany and Umbria as Orvieto, Perugia and Florence; the total travel time from Leonardo da Vinci to Florence is less than three hours.

B

BICYCLE HIRE

The stunning countryside of Tuscany and Umbria is prime cycling terrain, and there are rental outlets in a large number of cities and towns. Local tourist boards also provide a wealth of information on this popular Italian pastime.

In Florence, bicycles can be hired at low prices at the stand located in front of the Santa Maria Novella station (and at other locations) through an initiative (see page 133) set up to complement public transport, and ridden in the bicycle lanes throughout the city centre. In Lucca, where the bicycle is the most popular form of transport, you will find a rental company, Chronò (www.chronobikes.com), on Corso Garibaldi.

A useful English-language website on cycling in Florence and Tuscany is www.florencebikepages.com. For the really keen, there is even a chain of hotels tailored to cyclists: www.italybikehotels.com.

BUDGETING FOR YOUR TRIP

When determining your budget, think of Florence and the rest of Tuscany and Umbria as two separate entities. Florence is expensive, while the rest of Tuscany and Umbria is more moderate in terms of cost. In Florence, for example, you can expect to pay €120 to €180 for standard double-room accommodation. Outside Florence, you can probably find the same room for €70 to €120.

However, meals are not terribly expensive in Florence or anywhere else in Tuscany and Umbria. Depending on where you eat, of course, you can usually enjoy an excellent meal for two (excluding wine) for about €60; pizza or a salad for lunch will be about half that. Museum entry fees (and those for churches in Florence) are in the €2.50–€8 range, with tickets for museums in Florence sometimes costing over €15. Bus fares are lower than in most European cities, usually not much more than €1 per ticket.

C

CAMPING

Camping is permitted only in designated areas – usually crowded and not particularly appealing spots. The two campsites nearest Florence are notable exceptions: Camping Village Internazionale Firenze (Via San Cristofano, Impruneta; www.campinginternazionalefirenze.com) is a wooded park on the banks of the Arno; Camping Village Panoramico (www.campingpanoramicofiesole.com) is a very beautiful campsite on a hillside above Florence on Via Peramonda in Fiesole. Tourist information offices (see page 133) include campgrounds in their accommodation listings. A helpful website is www.camping.it.

CAR HIRE

One sure way to save money when hiring a car in Italy is to make arrangements before leaving home. All major companies have outlets in Italy and provide very competitive rates, especially for rentals of a week or more. A tax of 19 percent is added to all car rentals, and you may incur a surcharge of 10 percent if you pick up and drop off your car at the airport.

The minimum age required to hire a car in Italy is 18 and the driver must have held a license for at least a year.

Hertz: Via Borgo Ognisssanti 137, Florence; tel: 055 239 8205; www.hertz it

Europe Car: Via Borgo Ognissanti 53-55, Florence; tel: 055 290 431; www.europecar.co.uk

Avis: Via Borgo Ognissanti 128, Florence; tel: 055 213 629; www.avis.co.uk

CLIMATE

Tuscany and Umbria are not given to great extremes of climate, although it can be hot (especially in low-lying areas) in July and August. A hillside offering cooler temperatures and a refreshing breeze is never too far away, however; in August, there can be several degrees' difference in temperature between Florence and nearby hilltop Fiesole. Winters are chilly but rarely bitterly cold, and snow is pretty much confined to the highest hills. Spring is long (March to May) and very pleasant, while autumn is pleasantly mild but can be rainy.

Approximate monthly temperatures in Florence are as follows:

	J	F	M	A	M	J	J	A	S	O	N	D
max °C	9	12	16	20	24	29	32	31	28	21	14	10
min °C	2	2	5	8	12	15	17	17	15	11	6	3
max °F	48	54	61	68	75	84	90	88	82	70	57	50
min °F	36	36	41	46	54	59	63	63	59	52	43	37

CLOTHING

Italians like to dress well, and they will treat you with a little more respect if you dress smartly, too. In the spring and autumn, you will need a sweater or two and a raincoat, and in the winter it's best to dress warmly, as many buildings are old and draughty. Only the most expensive restaurants require jacket-and-tie formality, but you will want to dress well, even if casually so, for dinner. Shorts and sleeveless T-shirts are not considered proper clothing for a church visit – in fact, at some churches an attendant is posted at the front door to check for immodest attire.

CRIME AND SAFETY

Tuscany and Umbria are relatively safe, though pickpocketing and purse-snatching are now commonplace in Florence. Some common heists are those perpetrated by gypsy children or women carrying babies, who surround you and create a distracting commotion while cleaning out your

I want to report a theft.**Voglio denunciare un furto.**
My wallet/passport/ticket has been stolen. **Mi hanno rubato il portafoglio/il passaporto/il biglietto.**

pockets. Vespa-riding bandits, who snatch purses while whizzing by at high speed, are also a menace. If a theft occurs, make a statement at the police station within 24 hours if you want to make an insurance claim.

D

DISABLED TRAVELLERS

Despite difficult cobbled streets and poor wheelchair access to many tourist attractions and hotels, many people with disabilities visit Florence and Tuscany every year.

However, unaccompanied visitors will usually experience some difficulty, so it is best to travel with a companion.

Conditions and disability awareness are improving slowly in Tuscany (as well as in Italy in general), although the situation is certainly not ideal, and access is not always easy. More museums now have lifts, ramps and adapted toilets; newer trains and buses are accessible (although wheelchair users may need help when boarding); and recent laws require restaurants, bars and hotels to provide the relevant facilities. These laws, however, do not always cover access to those facilities. Information about the facilities offered at sights and museums is provided at tourist information centres. A lot of information is also available online at www.visit-tuscany.com in the Accessible Tourism section.

The Accessible Guide to Florence, by Cornelia Danielson, provides very detailed information on museums, restaurants, hotels and more for disabled travellers to Florence. Also, visit www.sagetraveling.com, the site of the European Disabled Travel Experts, tel: (+44)) 2035-406 155 (UK), +1-888-645 7920 (US), where you can order bespoke comprehensive guides to Florence, Siena, Livorno and the Tuscany region.

For drivers with disabilities, there are plenty of reserved parking places in towns, and these are free.

In the UK, you can obtain further information from Disability Rights UK, Plexal, East Bay Lane 14, London E20 3BS; tel: 0330-995 0400; www.disabilityrightsuk.org. In the US, contact SATH, tel: 212-447 7284; www.sath.org.

DRIVING

Central Italy's roads are well marked and meticulously maintained. The major hazards are your fellow motorists, who tend to drive fast and often recklessly. Two words of advice: drive defensively.

Drive on the right and pass on the left. At junctions and roundabouts, traffic on the right has the right of way. Drivers and passengers must wear seat belts, and motorcyclists must wear helmets. All cars must be equipped with a red warning triangle and a bright orange vest for the driver to wear in the road in case of breakdown. If you bring a car from the UK or Ireland you must adjust the headlights for right-side driving.

Italy's major motorways, *autostrade*, are four- to six-lane toll roads on which the maximum speed (rarely observed) is 130km/h (80mph). The A1, Autostrada del Sole, cuts through Tuscany and Umbria on its run up the peninsula from Naples to Milan, providing a quick connection with Rome and the rest of the country. On this and other *autostrade*, machines dispense tickets at the entrances; when you exit you pay the toll for the distance you've travelled. Tolls tend to be high – for up-to-date information on toll fees and the motorway network, visit www.autostrade.it.

The speed limit on secondary roads is 90km/h (55mph); in towns, it's 50km/h (30mph). In case of an accident or breakdown, dial 113 (your call will probably be answered by someone who does not speak English) or the Automobile Club of Italy on 116 (where your call may be answered by an English-speaker). Roadside phones, usually yellow, are placed at frequent intervals along major roads. And rest assured, any Italian driver who stops to assist you is likely to have a mobile phone, even if you don't.

It is usually difficult (and often illegal) to park on the street in urban areas. Look at signs carefully – parking is often restricted to residents only, or you have to pay at a kerbside machine, which will deliver a receipt (indicating the expiry time) that you must display on the dashboard. Many cities and towns have municipal car parks and garages at the fringes of their historic centres; use these whenever possible. Florence is ringed by parking facilities from which shuttle buses transport visitors into the centre.

E

ELECTRICITY

220V/50Hz is standard. Visitors from other countries may require an adaptor *(una presa complementare)*, and those from North America will need a converter as well. Better hotels often have special outlets for some North American appliances.

EMBASSIES AND CONSULATES

These offices are the places to go if you lose your passport, are embroiled in police or other bureaucratic dealings, or are otherwise in need of assistance. The US Consulate in Florence is at Lungarno Amerigo Vespucci 38, tel: (055) 266 951; https://it.usembassy.gov/embassy-consulates/florence. Citizens of other English-speaking countries can turn to their embassies in Rome:

Australia: Via Antonio Bosio 5, tel: (06) 852 721, www.italy.embassy.gov.au
Canada: Via Zara 30, tel: (06) 85444, www.canadainternational.gc.ca
New Zealand: Via Clitunno 44, tel: (06) 853 7501, www.mfat.govt.nz/en/embassies
Republic of Ireland: Villa Spada, Via Giacomo Medici 1, tel: (06) 585 2381, www.embassyofireland.it
South Africa: Via Tanaro 14, tel: (06) 852 541, www.sudafrica.it
UK: Via XX Settembre 80a, tel: (06) 4220 0001, www.ukinitaly.fco.gov.uk

EMERGENCIES

The general emergency number is 113. Call 112 for the *carabinieri* (national police), 115 for the fire brigade and 118 for an ambulance.

> police **alla polizia**
> fire brigade **ai pompieri**
> Fire! **Al fuoco!**

G

GETTING THERE

By air. Travellers from the UK have many options for flights to Tuscany and Umbria. Alitalia (www.alitalia.com) and British Airways (www.britishairways.com) offer regular flights to Florence from London and both also serve Pisa from London. Between them low-cost airlines Ryanair (www.ryanair.com) and easyJet (www.easyjet.com) also offer flights from London and other British cities to Pisa and Rome, as well as flights to Bologna, Perugia and Ancona.

From North America, Australia, New Zealand or South Africa, you can either fly into Rome's Leonardo da Vinci Airport and make air or land connections from there, or make a connecting flight in another European city before flying into central Italy. (Rome is preferable to Milan as it is closer and the connection between international and domestic flights in Milan requires a time-consuming change of airports.) North American travellers also have the additional option of taking advantage of the direct Delta (www.delta.com) flight from New York to Pisa. Alitalia, Delta, American Airlines (www.americanairlines.co.uk) and United (www.united.com) are among the major carriers that fly between the United States and Rome. Air Canada (www.aircanada.com) provides a service to Rome from major Canadian cities, while flights from Australia and New Zealand generally have a stopover in Hong Kong or Bangkok. South African Airways (www.flysaa.com) and Alitalia provide frequent services between Johannesburg and Rome, usually with a stopover in another European city.

By train. A sophisticated rail network links Italy with countries throughout Europe. If you are adding Tuscany and Umbria to a sojourn elsewhere in Europe, you will find that many international trains make stops in Florence and Pisa. The Eurostar service has considerably decreased travel times from London to Italy; on the most direct route, you can make the 2.5-hour trip to Paris and then connect to an overnight train to Pisa or Florence (a trip of 8–10 hours). Another option is to connect in Paris to one of the new high-speed trains that whisk you to Milan in just under 7 hours, and from there make connections to Florence (another 3 hours). For timetables and general information, contact the Ferrovia della Stato (FS, the Italian state railway), which has an informative website at www.fsitaliane.it. Another good source of information is www.voyages-sncf.com.

Budget options. If you are planning extensive rail travel in Europe, consider one of many available rail passes. A Eurail Global pass (available only to travellers who do not reside in a European country) allows unlimited travel through 28 European countries (the UK is a notable exception) for periods of 15 days–3 months, or for 5–7 days within a one-month period, or for 10–15 days within a two-month period; and the Eurail Select pass combines three to five bordering countries (check www.eurail.com). But if you simply want to get from one city to another, it may be considerably less expensive to pur-chase a one-way ticket. For information in the US contact Eurail (see above).

Europeans can buy an InterRail Pass, which is available in a variety of validity periods and allows for travel in 30 countries. For information, see www.interrail.eu/en.

By car. Italy is connected to the rest of Europe by an excellent road net-work. Even the trip to and from the UK has become much easier since the launch of the high-speed rail link under the channel that connects Folkstone with Calais (www.eurotunnel.com). Cars and passengers are whisked through the tunnel in 35 minutes; the service runs around the clock with departures every half-hour and sometimes more frequently.

GUIDES AND TOURS

Agencies specialising in tours of every corner of Tuscany and Umbria abound. Tourist offices and hotels can provide lists of these companies. In Florence, Florence Guides, an organisation of professional tourist guides authorised by the city council, includes many English-speaking

We'd like an English-speaking guide. **Ho bisogno di un guida che parla inglese.**

native Florentines who delight in introducing visitors to their city. Details of their tours can be found at the website, www.florenceguides.com. Another company is Context, which offers mini-seminars and city walks with international scholars specialised in areas like art, architecture and social history. Its website outlines the walks on offer and also features an interesting blog, www.contexttravel.com.

Many tours to the region include some interesting educational opportunities. Some language programmes that welcome students of all ages for courses from two weeks to several months are the British Institute of Florence, Piazza Strozzi 2, 50123 Firenze, tel: (055) 267 781, www.british institute.it, and the Università per Stranieri, Piazza Fortebraccio 4, 06122 Perugia, tel: (075) 57 461, www.unistrapg.it. Shaw Guides are a good source of information on educational holidays; visit www.shawguides.com.

H

HEALTH AND MEDICAL CARE

The good news is that, in terms of health, Tuscany and Umbria are among the safest places on earth to travel. You are not likely to encounter any unusual strains of infectious ailments, and health care is good.

Travellers from other EU countries should carry a European Health Insurance Card, which entitles them to free treatment; in the UK, consult the NHS website www.ehic.org.uk. US visitors who are not covered by their existing insurance when travelling abroad can purchase additional travel insurance (check with your insurance carrier about this optional coverage). You will often be asked to pay for treatment upfront,

I need a doctor/dentist. **Ho bisogno di un medico/dentista.**
I have a stomach-ache. **Ho mal di stomaco.**
I have a fever. **Ho la febre.**
I have sunstroke. **Ho un colpo di sole.**

so keep all receipts. A good source for information on health concerns is the International Association for Medical Assistance to Travellers (IAMAT). Consult www.iamat.org for details.

Because of the large volume of foreign travellers, Florence has created a special tourist Medical Service, located at Via Roma 4, tel: (055) 475 411.

Pharmacies *(farmacie)* have green crosses above the entrance; in each town one pharmacy stays open late and on Sunday on a rotating basis, and the after-hours locations for the month are posted in all pharmacy windows. The pharmacy in the Santa Maria Novella train station in Florence is open 24 hours a day.

Water is considered safe to drink, though Italians prefer bottled water, which is very inexpensive, and travellers from abroad may be wise to follow their example.

I

INTERNET

Italians are very internet savvy. In the larger cities like Florence, Pisa and Siena you will find free Wi-Fi points everywhere you go and the service is still expanding; but even the smaller towns are adapting quickly.

L

LGBTQ TRAVELLERS

Italians (especially in the north) tend to accept homosexuality but, still rooted in family traditions, may not tolerate public displays of affection. On the other hand, this is a country where friends of the same sex often walk down the street arm-in-arm, so there's quite a bit of latitude about what constitutes such a display. Florence is one of the most gay-friendly cities in Italy, and Elba one of the most popular resorts with the LGBTQ community; the latter has some *spiagge gay* (gay beaches). Azione Gay e Lesbica, Italy's national gay organisation, has an office in Florence at Via Pisana 32r, tel: (055) 220 250; you can check its website, which has listings of bars, bookshops and other resources throughout Italy, at www.azionegayelesbica.it.

M

MAPS

Tourism offices offer free maps of the historic centre in most cities. For a good road map, check out the frequently updated Touring Club of Italy's Tuscany and Umbria maps, available in local bookstores, as well as Insight Guides Flexi Map Tuscany

MEDIA

Florence's most popular newspaper is *La Nazione* – it publishes regional versions for most Tuscan towns. Other papers include La Repubblica and Corriere della Sera. English language magazines are hard to find but major international newspapers are usually available the day after publication.

MONEY

Currency. Italy uses the euro, divided into 100 cents. Notes come in denominations of €500, €200, €100, €50, €20, €10 and €5. There are coins for €2 and €1, and for 50, 20, 10, 5, 2 and 1 cent.

Currency exchange. Banks, which are generally open Mon–Fri 8.30am–1pm and 3–4pm (some open Sat morning in tourist areas), are a good option for currency exchange, despite their inconvenient hours. Major banks in cities and at least one bank in most towns have currency exchanges. Train stations and post offices also usually have currency exchange windows.

Credit cards. Credit cards are widely accepted. No one accepts travellers cheques anymore other than at an American Express office. Visa and MasterCard are the most widely accepted credit cards, and many establishments do not take American Express cards.

ATM machines. These usually offer more favourable exchange rates than

currency exchange offices. It's a good idea to check your bank's policies regarding withdrawal fees and daily limits before you leave home.

O

OPENING HOURS

Many museums remain open continuously throughout the day. Shops tend to close at lunchtime for two or more hours. The following can vary in some cities and towns.

Banks: 8.30am–1pm and 3–4pm, Mon–Fri (Sat morning in some areas).

Bars: 7am–11pm, often as late as 2am (many bars also serve food).

Churches: Very early in the morning until 12.30pm and 3–6 or 7pm (they open every day but discourage visits during mass).

Museums: six days a week, often 10am–6pm, or the same hours with a midday closure from 12.30–3pm.

Restaurants: 12.30–2.30 or 3pm for lunch, 7.30pm–10.30pm for dinner (they usually close one day a week).

Shops: 9am–1pm and 3.30 or 4pm–7 or 8pm.

P

POLICE

There are three kinds of police in Italy: *vigili urbani*, who deal with petty crime, traffic, parking and other day-to-day matters (including the concerns of tourists asking for directions); *carabinieri*, the highly trained national force who handle serious crime and civilian unrest, protect government figures and perform other high-profile tasks; and *polizia stradale*, who patrol the roadways. Any of these forces may

Where's the nearest police station? **Dovè il più vicino posto di polizia?**

answer a 113 emergency call, though the *carabinieri* have their own emergency number, 112. The main police station in Florence is at Via Pietrapiana 50r.

POST OFFICES

Generally post offices are open Mon–Fri 8am–1.30pm and Sat 8.15am–12.30pm. Stamps can be bought from post offices or from tobacconists. Whatever you send and however long you travel, chances are you will be back home long before it reaches its destination. If you want something to arrive with alacrity, consider using FedEx, www.fedex.com/it, or another international delivery service.

Many post offices also exchange money. Post boxes mostly red, normally set in the wall and marked with Poste.

> I would like a stamp for this letter/postcard. **Vorrei un francobollo per questa lettera/cartolina.**

PUBLIC HOLIDAYS

Tuscany and Umbria celebrate many local festivals *(see page 97)*, as well as all the national holidays. These are:

1 January New Year's Day
6 January Epiphany
March/April Easter Sunday and Monday
25 April Liberation Day
1 May Labour Day
2 June Republic Day
15 August Ferragosto and Assumption Day
1 November All Saints' Day
8 December Day of the Immaculate Conception
25 December Christmas
26 December St Stephen's Day

T

TELEPHONES

Public phone boxes, which are phone-card-operated, are becoming harder and harder to find. Pre-paid phonecards are available from tobacconists, newsstands and some bars. Italian area codes begin with a '0'. Dial the full area code (e.g. 055 for Florence), even for a local call. For international calls dial 00, then the country code, then the city or area code, without the '0' (except for mobile numbers), then the number. Foreign mobile-phone users must dial the international access code even when calling an Italian number from within Italy (00 39). To avoid hotel surcharges on international calls, use a call card issued by BT and AT&T among other companies.

Almost all mobile phones should work in Italy; to make sure, check to see if yours supports GSM900 and GSM1800 frequencies. It can be expensive to use your mobile abroad – before you go check with your provider on how to arrange cheaper calls. Alternatively, particularly if you are staying longer, consider swapping your SIM card for an Italian SIM, obtainable from cell phone shops.

TIME ZONES

GMT plus 1 hour in winter, plus 2 hours in summer. Clocks are advanced one hour in April and turned back one hour in October.

TIPPING

A 15 percent service charge is added to most restaurant bills, but a little extra for good service is appreciated. Tip bellboys €1 per bag. Taxi drivers: round up the fare to the nearest euro and add one more.

TOILETS

Public toilets can be hard to find, and you usually have to pay to use one. Facilities in stations are often poorly maintained. For the price of a coffee you can use the toilet in a bar. The gents' is designated by *uomini* or *signori*, the ladies' by *donne* or *signore*.

TOURIST INFORMATION

Italian National Tourist Office (ENIT; www.enit.it) offices include:

Canada: 365 Bay Street, Suite 503, Toronto, Ontario M5H 2V1, tel: (416) 925 4882, email: toronto@enit.it.

UK: 1 Princes Street, London W1B 2AY, tel: (020) 7408 1254, email: info.london@enit.it.

US: 686 Park Avenue, New York, NY 10065, tel: (212) 245 5618, email: newyork@enit.it; 401 N. Michigan Avenue, Suite 172, Chicago, IL 60611, tel: (312) 644 9335, email: chicago@enit.it; 1085 Wilshire Boulevard, Suite 575, Los Angeles, CA 90024, tel: (310) 820 1898, email: losangeles@enit.it.

Italy: Regional tourist offices: Tuscany: Via Vittorio Emanuele II, Firenze, tel: (055) 462 801; Umbria: Corso Vannucci 96, Perugia, tel: (075) 5041

Many towns have tourist offices that can often provide detailed information that is not available from regional tourist offices.

Piazza del Comune 12, Assisi, tel: (075) 812 534

Via Cavour 1r, Firenze, tel. (055) 290 832, www.firenzeturismo.it

Via della Repubblica 15, Gubbio, tel: (075) 922 0693

Via Carducci 10, Lucca, tel: (0584) 962 233, www.luccaturismo.it

Piazza Don Minzoni 1, Montepulciano, tel: (0578) 757 341

Piazza del Duomo 24, Orvieto, tel. (0763) 341 772

Piazza Matteotti 18, Perugia, tel: (075) 573 6458

Piazza Duomo 7, Pisa, tel: 050 550 100, www.turismo.pisa.it

Piazza Buonamici 7, Prato, tel: 0574 24112, www.pratoturismo.it

Piazza Duomo 1, Siena, tel: (0577) 280 551, www.terresiena.it

Piazza della Libertà 7, Spoleto, tel: (0743) 238 920

TRANSPORT

An extensive public transport network makes it easy to move between major cities and towns without a car, although having your own transport does make it easier to visit the delightful rustic settings for which the regions are famous. Tourist offices will usually provide bus and train timetables and fare information; in fact, if you explain where you want to go and when, staff will usually look up times for you. Timetables are posted at train stations and can be consulted at the automated ticket machines. Stamp your ticket in one of the machines on the platform before boarding the train; you may be heavily fined if you don't.

Florence, Perugia, Siena, Pisa and other cities in Tuscany and Umbria (and even many small towns as well) have excellent local bus systems. Tickets can be purchased at newsstands and generally cost around €1.20. Most bus systems offer 24-hour tickets and multi-day passes, which give a small discount. Stamp your ticket in one of the machines when you board the bus; failure to do so can result in a hefty fine. Florence is one of the many Italian cities implementing a bicycle-sharing system (Mobike) to complement the public transport system. Riders can buy daily and weekly passes for access to the various bike deposits throughout the city. The first of three tram lines being constructed in Florence is now up and running.

When is the next bus/train to...? **Quando parte il prossimo autobus/treno per...?**
one way **andata**
round trip **andata e ritorno**
first/second class **prima/seconda classe**
What's the fare to...? **Qual è la tariffa per...?**

V

VISAS AND ENTRY REQUIREMENTS

Citizens of EU countries need only a valid passport or identity card to enter Italy. Citizens of the US, Canada, Australia, New Zealand and South Africa need only a valid passport, although a special visa or residence permit is required for stays of more than 90 days. To facilitate the replacement process in case you lose your passport while travelling, take photocopies of your passport; leave one copy at home, and keep another with you, but separately from the passport.

Currency restrictions. While there is no limit on the amount of currency you can bring into Italy, you must declare any currency over the amount of €10,000 upon leaving the country if travelling to a country outside the EU.

IVA. A Value Added Tax of 23 percent is added to all purchases in Italy. In many cases, residents of non-EU countries can claim a refund for part of this tax on purchases over a certain amount at one shop – if they are willing to follow some complex procedures. There's lots of good, straightforward advice (specific to Italy) on the English-language pages of www.agenziadoganemonopoli.gov.it/portale/ee/citizen/vta-refund.

W

WEBSITES

The following is a list of helpful English-language websites.
www.firenzemusei.it: ticketing website for Florence's State museums and exhibits
www.visitflorence.com: up-to-date information about Florence
www.mugellotoscana.it: Mugello valley information
www.perugiaonline.com: Perugia tourism information
www.assisionline.com: Assisi tourism information
www.orvietoonline.com: Orvieto tourism information
www.welcometuscany.it: up-to-date information on Tuscany
www.visittuscany.com: Tuscany Tourism Office official site
www.umbriatourism.it: Umbria Tourist Board official site
www.accessibleitaly.com: useful website for travellers with disabilities

Y

YOUTH HOSTELS

There are hostels in Florence, Perugia, Lucca and some other towns. The Associazione Italiana Alberghi per la Gioventù (AIG) can provide a list of hostels and a free booking service. AIG, Viale Mazzini 88, 00195 Roma, tel: (06) 9826 1462, www.aighostels.it, email: info@aighostels.it.

RECOMMENDED HOTELS

Our selective list of hotels below includes those that have a good amount of character, are well located, provide excellent value for the price, or in some other way are above the ordinary.

Reservations are essential almost anywhere in the regions from May to September, and are highly recommended at other times, especially around European holidays. Florence City Council applies a 'Tourism Tax' to visitors staying in any overnight accommodation within the city; it is the responsibility of the accommodation providers to collect this (ranging from €2–5 per person, per night).

As a basic indication of what you can expect to pay, we use the euro symbol below to indicate prices for a double room with bath, including breakfast – but remember that prices may vary with the season. For additional hotels in Florence, consult the *Berlitz Pocket Guide to Florence*.

€€€€	over 250 euros
€€€	170–250 euros
€€	100–170 euros
€	below 100 euros

FLORENCE

Hotel Brunelleschi €€€€ *Piazza Santa Elisabetta 3, 50122 Firenze, tel: (055) 27 370*, www.brunelleschihotelflorence.com. Built into a Byzantine tower, this smart hotel offers modern amenities and tasteful décor; some rooms have canopied beds. It is tucked away in a tiny, quiet piazza just a short walk from the Duomo. There are delightful views from the Belvedere Terrace. 96 rooms.

Hotel Davanzati €€ *Via Porta Rossa 5, 50123 Firenze, tel: (055) 286 666*, www.hoteldavanzati.it. Named for its proximity to the Palazzo Davanzati, this hotel offers good value. Its clean, quiet rooms are all equipped with laptops and internet access. 19 rooms.

Hotel Tornabuoni Beacci €€€€ *Via Tornabuoni 3, 50123 Firenze, tel: (055) 212 645,* www.tornabuonihotels.com. This lovely, atmospheric hotel near the Arno is over 80 years old, and has the air of a well-heeled *pensione*, though it is a well-run, full-service hotel. Public areas include a reading room organised around a large fireplace, and the guest rooms are furnished with comfortable old pieces that look as though they have been passed down through the generations. The roof garden affords views over tiled rooftops to the hills. Bar and restaurant. 28 rooms.

Il Guelfo Bianco €€ *Via Cavour 29, 50129 Firenze, tel: (055) 288 330,* www.ilguelfobianco.it. This efficiently run hotel is located on a busy thoroughfare between the Duomo and the Piazza San Marco. A cellar-to-rooftop renovation rendered the décor here more or less contemporary, giving the premises the look of a comfortable big-city establishment. Enough of the original detailing remains to remind you that this hotel occupies a 15th-century palace. 40 rooms.

J&J €€€ *Via di Mezzo 20, 50121 Firenze, tel: (055) 26 312,* www.jandjhotel. net. This pleasant little hotel is located on a quiet, non-touristy street to the northeast side of the city centre. It is set in a Renaissance palace and retains some of the original frescoes and vaulted ceilings. Each bedroom is decorated differently, and some of them open onto a communal courtyard. 21 rooms.

Rezidenza Johanna 1 €€ *Via Bonifacio Lupi 14, 50129 Firenze, tel: (055) 481 896,* www.johanna.it. The owners at this charming residence have created a homely, laid-back atmosphere. The bedrooms are quite roomy and beautifully furnished and there is a cosy communal room where guests can help themselves to a drink. Located on the northern edge of the city near Piazza San Marco. 11 rooms.

REST OF TUSCANY
Arezzo

Continentale €€ *Piazza Guido Monaco 7, 52100 Arezzo, tel: (0575) 20 251,* www.hotelcontinentale.com. Arezzo is an extremely pleasant place to stop for a night, perhaps if you are on a swing through southern Tuscany on your way to Umbria. The Continentale is definitely the choice place to stay, especially as it has a central location close to the railway station and the major attractions of the Old City. The bedrooms and suites are individually decorated, and some have a private terrace. 73 rooms.

Cortona

San Michele €€ *Via Guelfa 15, 52044 Cortona, tel: (0575) 604 348*, www.cortonaluxuryaccommodation.com/sanmichele. Lovely, medieval Cortona deserves a hotel like this, occupying a 15th-century palazzo and providing welcoming accommodation of the vaulted-ceiling and exposed-timber variety. The best room in the house commands a bird's-eye view of the town and valley below from a tower. 40 rooms.

Fiesole

Pensione Bencista €€ *Via Benedetto da Maiano 4, 50014 Fiesole, tel: (055) 59 163*, www.bencista.com. Just down the hill from the Villa San Michele this lovely *pensione* offers the same views and the same refreshing breezes at a fraction of the cost, and also provides a delightful *en famille* ambiance. The building dates from the 14th century and has a pretty garden and large, rambling guest rooms filled with antiques and other comfortable furnishings. The rates include breakfast but half board is also available. 44 rooms.

Villa San Michele €€€€ *Via Doccia 4, 50014 Fiesole, tel: (055) 567 8200*, www.villasanmichele.com. You may feel like one of the Medici when staying in this luxurious 15th-century villa, with a facade designed by Michelangelo, high in the hills above Florence. While such amenities as a heated swimming pool, luxuriant gardens and princely guest rooms come at a price that can make a dent in the largest coffers, a stay here is an extraordinary experience. Closed low season. 45 rooms.

Lucca

La Luna € *Via Fillungo–Corte Compagni 12, 55100 Lucca, tel: (0583) 493 634*, www.hotellaluna.it. Two renovated wings of a centuries-old building are the setting for this great-value hotel. Most rooms face a courtyard, with pleasant if rather bland contemporary furnishings, although a few still retain the character of days gone by. Parking available for guests. 29 rooms.

Montepulciano

Il Marzocco € *Piazza Savonarola 18, 53045 Montepulciano, tel: (0578) 757 262, www.albergoilmarzocco.it.* You may think you've stumbled into the Italy of years gone by when you enter this old-fashioned hotel on a medieval piazza inside the town walls. The building is 16th-century, but most of the furnishings are from the 19th century. The best rooms are those with terraces overlooking the countryside. 16 rooms.

Pisa

Royal Victoria € *Lungarno Pacinotti 12, 56126 Pisa, tel: (050) 940 111, www.royalvictoria.it.* Everything about this comfortable old hotel reeks of character, from a location beside the Arno to the antiques-filled public rooms, to the idiosyncratic guest rooms. Some of these are furnished with heavy 19th-century pieces, some are frescoed, some have a 1920s appearance. 48 rooms.

Prato

Charme Hotel € *Via delle Badie 228, 50047 Prato, tel: (0574) 550 541, www.charmehotel.it.* Prato is an excellent alternative if you can't find a hotel in Florence. The Charme Hotel is located in a tranquil part of town. The rooms are clean and modern, and the hotel also offers a sauna, fitness room and large parking lot. A good choice for practical travellers with their own transport, who are looking for a good deal in the vicinity of Florence. 72 rooms.

San Gimignano

La Cisterna €€ *Piazza della Cisterna 23, 53037 San Gimignano, tel: (0577) 940 328, www.hotelcisterna.it.* This is one of San Gimignano's most atmospheric inns. It occupies the lower portions of two 14th-century towers and faces an attractive piazza. Many rooms, which are plainly but tastefully furnished, have views across tiled rooftops to the countryside; others look onto the town's medieval lanes. 50 rooms.

Leon Bianco € *Piazza della Cisterna 13, 53037 San Gimignano, tel: (0577) 941 294, www.leonbianco.com.* Rivalling La Cisterna *(see above)* for charm, this pleasant inn, the White Lion, also occupies a centuries-old building, this one an 11th-century palazzo that has been tastefully restored, and faces the same lovely square as its neighbour. Here, too, rooms are pleasant and cosy, and most afford alluring vistas of the town or countryside. 25 rooms.

Siena

Antica Torre € *Via Fieravecchia 7, 53100 Siena, tel: (0577) 222 255, www.anticatorresiena.it.* A 17th-century tower located in a quiet corner of the city (but just a short walk from the centre) is the setting for this delightful and friendly little hotel. The guest rooms are small but tastefully decorated with handsome old pieces of furniture, and are reached by way of an enchanting stone staircase. 8 rooms.

Duomo €€ *Via Stalloreggi 38, 53100 Siena, tel: (0577) 289 088, www.hotelduomo.it.* The location is the main attraction here. Set on the top floor of a centuries-old building near the Campo and the Cathedral, the Duomo makes a perfect base from which to enjoy the city. The upper-floor setting affords stunning views of the city's towers and the countryside. The rooms are pleasant, with contemporary furnishings, and some have balconies. 20 rooms.

Volterra

San Lino €€ *Via San Lino 26, 56048 Volterra, tel: (0588) 85 250, www.hotelsanlino.net.* Set in a 15thcentury convent, with guest rooms created in what were the nuns' dormitories, the San Lino hotel offers numerous up-to-date comforts that include chic contemporary furnishings, air-conditioning, minibars, a swimming pool, a courtyard garden and private parking for guests – all this, plus a nice location within the town walls. Be aware, though, when making your reservation, that the superior rooms are far more superior than the standard rooms. 43 rooms.

UMBRIA
Assisi

Hotel Berti € *Piazza S. Pietro, 06081 Assisi, tel: (075) 813 466,* www.hotel berti.it. Just 200m from the Basilica of St Francis, this cosy hotel is very convenient for exploring the city. The staff are friendly and the hotel is connected to restaurant Da Cecco, which makes it easy to grab a quick meal after a day's sightseeing. There is a courtyard garden where breakfast can be served in summer. 10 rooms.

Umbra €€ *Vicolo degli Archi 6, 06081 Assisi, tel: (075) 812 240,* www.hotel umbra.it. You may think you have found the getaway of your dreams when you arrive at this lovely 13th-century palazzo. There's a wonderful, old-fashioned feeling throughout, from the medieval vaults and brickwork to the 19th- to early 20th-century pieces of furniture in the salons and guest rooms. Many rooms are suites, with sitting areas near windows providing views of tiled rooftops and the valley below. A grassy garden adjoins the superb restaurant. Panoramic rooftop terrace. 25 rooms.

Gubbio

Bosone Palace € *Via XX Settembre 22, 06024 Gubbio, tel: (075) 922 0688,* www.hotelbosone.com. Gubbio's best hotel may well provide the most atmospheric accommodation in Umbria, housed as it is in a 14th-century palazzo. Many of the spacious guest rooms are frescoed, and several suites are tastefully furnished with reproduction Renaissance pieces. 30 rooms.

Gattapone €€ *Via Beni 11, 06024 Gubbio, tel: (075) 927 2489,* www.hotel-gattapone.net. A renovation has left only the timbered ceilings and other architectural elements to remind you that these surroundings in the centre of town have seen the passage of many centuries. Furnishings, bathrooms and other facilities are completely up to date, and the views over the rooftops are enchanting. It is advisable to book well in advance. Wheelchair access. 18 rooms.

Orvieto

La Badia €€ *Loc. La Badia 8, 05018 Orvieto (3km/2 miles south of Orvieto), tel: (0763) 301 959, www.labadiahotel.it.* A 12th-century former monastery offers one of Umbria's most cherished country retreats. The guest rooms and suites vary in size considerably but all are very tasteful, with stone walls and beams. There are views towards graceful Orvieto atop its bluff which you can enjoy from a sun bed in the grounds, which have a pool and tennis courts and are very well maintained. Restaurant. 27 rooms.

Hotel Duomo €€ *Vicolo di Maurizio 7, 05018 Orvieto, tel: (0763) 341 887, www.orvietohotelduomo.com.* This centrally located hotel has an attractive courtyard and spacious, quiet rooms. The hotel is a showcase for the works of renowned local artist Livio Orazio Valentini. 18 rooms.

Perugia

Sangallo Palace €€ *Via Luigi Masi 9, 06121 Perugia, tel: (075) 573 0202), www.sangallo.it.* This large hotel stands in an enviable position, a short walk to a moving staircase that takes you up to *centro storico* via the Rocca Paolina (the mount on which the old town is built). Spacious individual rooms are decorated in classic style, and some have balconies with a view of Basilica di San Domenico. The welcoming staff are very knowledgeable. Other facilities include a car park below the hotel and an indoor swimming pool. 100 rooms.

Spoleto

Palazzo Leti – Residenza d'Epoca €€ *Via Filippo Brignone 13, 06049 Spoleto, tel: (0743) 224 930, www.palazzoleti.com.* From the moment you enter the courtyard and see the stunning views over the hillside you will be in awe of this hotel. The place is very tranquil with manicured gardens where you can relax. Each room is unique decorated in warm colours – some with wooden beams and vaulted ceilings. 12 rooms.

INDEX

INSIGHT ⊙ GUIDES POCKET GUIDE

TUSCANY & UMBRIA

First Edition 2018

Editor: Carine Tracanelli
Author: Stephen Brewer
Updaters: Jackie Staddon and Hilary Weston
Head of DTP and Pre-Press: Rebeka Davies
Picture Editor: Tom Smyth
Cartography Update: Carte
Photography Credits: Corners Images
Britta Jaschinski/Apa Publications 27, 28,
31, 33, 37, 39, 41, 42, 45, 70; Corbis 5TC,
16, 21, 34; Dreamstime 4TL, 18, 23, 65, 69,
75, 76, 79, 80, 82, 85, 91–93; Fotolia 57;
Hans Hofer/Apa Publications 29; iStock
4TC, 4MC, 4ML, 5T, 5M, 5MR, 6L, 6R, 7, 7,
66; Shutterstock 5MC; Steve MacDonald/
Apa Publications 4TL, 8L, 9, 11, 12, 14, 22,
51, 54, 59, 60, 71, 73, 86, 87, 91, 92, 94, 96,
99, 104, 106
Cover Picture: iStock

Distribution
UK, Ireland and Europe: Apa Publications
(UK) Ltd; sales@insightguides.com
United States and Canada: Ingram
Publisher Services; ips@ingramcontent.com
Australia and New Zealand: Woodslane;
info@woodslane.com.au
Southeast Asia: Apa Publications (SN) Pte;
singaporeoffice@insightguides.com
Worldwide: Apa Publications (UK) Ltd;
sales@insightguides.com

**Special Sales, Content Licensing
and CoPublishing**
Insight Guides can be purchased in bulk
quantities at discounted prices. We can
create special editions, personalised jackets
and corporate imprints tailored to your
needs. sales@insightguides.com;
www.insightguides.biz

All Rights Reserved
© 2018 Apa Digital (CH) AG and
Apa Publications (UK) Ltd

Printed in China by CTPS

Contact us
Every effort has been made to provide
accurate information in this publication,
but changes are inevitable. The publisher
cannot be responsible for any resulting loss,
inconvenience or injury. We would appreciate
it if readers would call our attention to any
errors or outdated information. We also
welcome your suggestions; please contact
us at: hello@insightguides.com
www.insightguides.com